P9-BHU-548

PARSHA PARABLES 3

Stories and anecdotes that shine a new light on the weekly Torah portion & holidays

By Rabbi Mordechai Kamenetzky

Parsha Parables 3
© Copyright 2000 by Bentsh Press
Second printing December 2000

All rights reserved. No part of this book may be reproduced in any form or with any technology, without express authorization from the publisher.

Hardcover ISBN: 0-9657697-2-0
Softcover ISBN: 0-9657697-3-9

Published by:
Bentsh Press
P.O. Box 224
Hewlett, NY 11557

Distributed by:
Feldheim Publishers
200 Airport Executive Park
Nanuet, NY 10954
(914) 356-2282

Designed and produced by:
Dynagrafik Design Studios
Cover by:
Spotlight Design, Inc.

Printed and bound in the United States of America by:
Noble Book Press Corp.

To order additional copies of this book,
please call (516) 374-7363 ext. 124
e-mail: rmk@torah.org

For all comments and suggestions,
please write:
Rabbi Mordechai Kamenetzky
P.O. Box 224
Hewlett, NY 11557
Fax: (516) 569-7954

אמר רבי יצחק

לא היה צריך להתחיל את התורה אלא מהחדש הזה לכם . . .

ומה טעם פתח בבראשית . . .

(רש"י בראשית א"א)

The Torah should have begun
with the laws of Rosh Chodesh....

*Oh! But how sweet a **ta'am** it has,*
now that it started with the stories of Braishis.

— Rabbi Levi Yizchak of Berditchev
in a homiletic interpretation

THE PARSHA PARABLES SERIES HAS LARGELY BEEN MADE POSSIBLE
THROUGH THE GENEROUS SUPPORT OF

KEREN MA'ASIM TOVIM

בס"ד

קרן מעשים טובים
KEREN MA'ASIM TOVIM

A teacher asks one of her pupils:

"What's the capital of the United States?"

"Washington, D.C.," comes the reply.

"And what does D.C. stand for?"

"Dot com," the pupil answers innocently.

Welcome to the dot.com generation, a world from which this work has risen, from faxes and e-mails to the old-fashioned method of disseminating knowledge — books in print.

Two years have passed since the publication of Rabbi Mordechai Kamenetzky's *More Parsha Parables.* While the level of *frumkeit* (religious awarness and commitment) seems on the rise, our *rabbeim* and educators must work harder to insure that *ehrlichkeit* (righteousness) keeps pace, so that no one should claim that *frumkeit* is ahead while *ehrlichkeit* lags behind. We have used technology to educate. Ah, if only ethical conduct would keep up with technology!

The *Medrash Rabba* in *Vayikrah* (Chapter 16:2) relates a story about a peddler who journeyed from town to town hawking his wares.

He loudly proclaimed, "Who wants to buy medication for long life?" Reb Yannai, upon hearing the announcement, invited the merchant to come over and sell him some of the potion. The merchant responded, "You do not need *my* medication. It is not meant for those like you." When Reb Yannai persisted, the merchant agreed to demonstrate the formula. He opened up a Sefer *Tehillim* and showed him the verse: "Who is the man who desires life and loves days of seeking good? Guard your tongue from evil and your lips from speaking deceit. Turn from evil and do good; seek peace and pursue it" (*Psalms* 34:14-16).

Reb Yannai was amazed. "All my life I read this verse and did not understand how simple it was until this merchant came along and taught it to me."

The Torah commentaries are all baffled by Reb Yannai's exclamation. What new interpretation did the merchant divulge to Reb Yannai that he did not already know from a lifetime of learning?

The *Shulchan Aruch* in *Orach Chaim* establishes a cardinal rule: "One must evaluate and assess all of one's actions and activities throughout the course of the day, and determine whether each individual deed is correct from a Torah perspective. Only then shall one proceed, and if not, he should refrain. Whoever lives his life in this manner is considered as if he were perpetually serving the Creator, as it is written, '*be'-chol d'rochecho do'ai'hoo*, in all your ways, you shall acknowledge Him' (*Proverbs* 3:6).

Accordingly, if even optional activities such as eating, drinking, walking, and other basic needs are performed with the thought of enhancing and facilitating the service of HaShem (e.g., eating, to be healthy; sleeping, to be rested; having children, to perpetuate our heritage), then they are a fulfillment of "serving Hashem in every capacity" *(Orach Chaim 231:1).*

I would like to extend this concept to the world of commerce. If one conducts his affairs ethically, guided by the words of Dovid *HaMelech,* "Guard your tongue from evil and your lips from speaking deceit;" and if his goal is to generate an honest income to raise his family, do *mitzvohs,* and act righteously, then one is serving Hashem even in a mundane setting.

This was the merchant's revelation: he was referring to himself as a simple businessman. One can be an "*ish he'chofetz chaim*, a seeker of life," not only by studying Torah all day, but even by conducting one's affairs ethically and righteously.

Previously, Reb Yannai thought that full-day service of Hashem only could be accomplished through full-day Torah study, as he was doing, and so he listened with bewilderment to the merchant's new explanation, which subsequently became codified as *halacha* in the *Shulchan Aruch*. Yes, a simple interpretation, but a powerful message!

Of course, this kind of "*be'chol d'rochecho do'ai'hoo*," all-encompassing awareness of Hashem, approach to life and leisure, vocation and vacation, requires discipline. It takes a full-course serving of a commitment to ethics and honesty, and perhaps a supplement of *Parsha Parables*.

Parsha Parables are not just enjoyable anecdotes that shine a new light on the weekly *parsha*. Each interpretation embraces ideals and principles sorely needed in our daily behavior, principles that are rooted in enduring Torah values. As such, the more you consume of *Parsha Parables*, the more it will become part of you, and catapult you to new heights of consciousness, righteousness, and rectitude.

The *Mishna* in *Avos* says, "Torah study is good together with *derech eretz*, for the exertion of them both makes sin forgotten" (*Avos* 2:2).

In Tractate Yoma 85b, *Tosfos Yeshanim* elucidates Rabbeinu Tam's position regarding the relationship of *derech eretz* to Torah study. He infers from the language of the *Mishna* that *derech eretz* takes precedence to Torah study, as is clearly noted in the statement, Torah is good with *derech eretz*, as if to say it is good to have Torah, together with the main course of *derech eretz*.

Other scholars disagree with Rabbeinu Tam. "How can this be the meaning of the *Mishna*, if the same *Mishna* continues, 'All Torah study that is not joined with work will cease in the end?'" Clearly, the inference from this section is that Torah study is foremost!

Furthermore, the *Mishna* in *Avos* (Chapter 6) which lists the 48 means of Torah achievement includes "limited business activity."

Rabbi Elchonon Wasserman, *zt"l*, provides a brilliant reconciliation of Rabbeinu Tam's position: The words *derech eretz* can assume two distinct meanings. *Derech eretz* can mean an occupation. It also can mean *midos tovos* and *ma'asim no'im*, good character and dignifying deeds.

Thus, the two *mishna*yos are referring to two distinct types of *derech eretz*. Accordingly, *derech eretz* that represents careers and livelihood should be limited; but the *derech eretz* of good character and dignifying deeds is a priority, even paramount to Torah study! The message is clear: *Ehrlichkeit* takes precedence to *frumkeit*!

A story comes to mind about the holy founder of *chassidus*, the Ba'al Shem Tov known by his acronym as the *Besht*. In the years before his revelation as a holy sage, Rabbi Yisroel Ba'al Shem Tov wandered from town to town, disguised as a homeless beggar, unknown to anyone. This practice, known as *golus,* was standard procedure for many *tzadikim.*

Whenever he arrived in one particular *shtetl*, he was ignored by almost everyone. Sitting alone after the Friday night *tefilos,* nobody except a Jew named Reb Avraham paid any attention to him. Reb Avraham, instantly recognized the wisdom, warmth, and originality personified by this *tzadik*, and always invited him to share *shabbos* meals with him.

Years later, as a world-renowned *tzadik* and chassidic master, the Ba'al Shem Tov once again passed through this *shtetl*.

This time, however, he traveled in a beautiful carriage pulled by four great horses skillfully managed by an experienced coachman. When the townspeople heard that the Ba'al Shem Tov was approaching their *shtetl*, they marched en masse to welcome the great chassidic leader. The affluent members of the community battled among themselves over who would merit hosting the revered guest. Finally, they agreed that the *Rosh Ha'Kohol* (community leader), the wealthiest man in town, would be the ideal host for this great sage.

The *Rosh Ha'Kohol* graciously invited the *tzaddik* to proceed to his beautiful mansion, but the *Besht* had other plans. He ordered his coachman to transport the carriage and the horses to the mansion, while he himself walked over to the home of his generous host in the lean years, Reb Avraham.

It didn't take long for the *Rosh Ha'Kohol* to realize that he would only be hosting the horses and carriage; the Ba'al Shem Tov would not be coming. And so the *Rosh Hakohol* came running, requesting an explanation.

The *Besht* explained, "I am the same person who came through this town on previous occasions. During those trips, no one but Reb Avraham was kind enough to offer his hospitality. So why does everyone want to host me now? It must be my elegant carriage and fine horses. So fine! You may act as the gracious host for my carriage and horses, while I will patronize my customary host."

Keren Ma'Asim Tovim thanks and congratulates Rabbi Mordechai Kamenetzky for allowing us to once again be the *achsanyah shel Torah*, a sponsor, a vehicle, through whose assistance these interesting parables and homiletic interpretations, "a new perspective of age-old themes," are disseminated to multitudes who are thirsty for Hashem's words.

"Opportunities must be seized or they will be lost," a caring President recently said. The *velt zogt* that people sometimes fail in life because they major in minor things. Helping Rabbi Kamenetzky, we are confident, is an opportunity seized, and a leap into the majors. It is an honor, a privilege, and a joy to be a part of this endeavor.

Rabbi Meir says in *Pirkei Avos* (Chapter 6:1), "*Kol haosek b'Torah lishmah, zoche ledvorim harbay,* whoever engages in Torah study for it's purest sake merits many things."

The *Chasam Sofer* notes that the word *devorim* literally means *words*, thus *zoche ledvorim harbay* can also mean *merits many words*. Our dear author, Reb Mordechai, is obviously a talented man of many words.

How does one merit the wonderful pedestal of many words? We need not search too far, for the *mishna* establishes the correlation: Who merits the lofty position of *zoche ledvorim har'bay*, where even his seemingly insignificant talk requires study? One who toils in Torah study purely out of love for it and devotion to its cause. As the Chinuch explains it: "The highest reward for a person's toil is not what he gets for it, but what he becomes by it."

Reb Mordechai became a *zoche ledvorim har'bay, k'pshuto u'k'medrosho*, in its simple meaning as well as in its homiletic interpretation; he is a man whose words reach out and touch the farthest corners of the land — and the innermost recesses of the heart.

On behalf of *Keren Ma'Asim Tovim*, I dedicate the publication of *Parsha Parables III* to my dear wife, Mindy, for, among other things, the tranquility and dedication that she brings to our home. We pray that the z'*chus* of the publication and dissemination of this *sefer* should help us be *zoche* to the blessings of *Chazal*, "*zochu, shechinah shruya beineihem,*" let the Divine Presence dwell among us, bless us, and safeguard us, *kain ye'hi ratzon,* and so may it be.

Avrohom Pinchos Berkowitz

Keren Ma'asim Tovim

Elul 5760

Dedicated in memory of

ר' ישראל בן יהודה ע"ה

Zoltan Honig

of blessed memory

His family's only male survivor of the Holocaust,
he replanted roots of faith, commitment
and kindness on these shores.

Generous and compassionate,
he raised a new generation
on a new continent
to continue the cherished traditions
of his holy heritage lost in the smoldering flames
of the Holocaust.

May his children and grandchildren
be a blessing to his sacred memory
as the roots of Yiddishkeit that he replanted
in this country continue to blossom
with fruit of *Torah, Avodah*
and *Gemilas Chassadim.*

Yehuda and Beth Honig
and Family

ישיבה דפילאדעלפיא

בס״ד

To My Dear Nephew,

Rabbi Mordechai Kamenetzky, whom I have loved since his youth, who spreads Torah at Yeshiva Ateres Yaakov. It is with a joyous heart that I greet you with blessings on the printing of your weekly Torah thoughts that are filled with sparks of insight.

I am sure that when a majority of a generation uses computers, there is an increased ability to touch the hearts of our brethren from far and near and bring them to their Father in Heaven. Now that these Torah thoughts will be printed in a book, I am sure that many more people will enjoy the *Divrei Torah* with a new look into the sanctity of Torah and the elevation of the soul.

I therefore bless you with my heart and soul to spread your ideas forward, that people may enjoy, grow and be inspired from the beautiful thoughts and words.

Affectionately,

Rabbi Shmuel Kamenetsky

Table of Contents

Introduction

Praising Parables

As much as I enjoy writing the weekly *FaxHomily,* I take pleasure in writing the Introduction to each book of the *Parsha Parable* Series. After all, it gives me a chance to offer a perspective of how the pressure to write a parable every week, and match it with a bona fide *d'var* Torah, makes me view the world through the various lenses of both an aspiring author, a quasi-philosopher, and even a student of the Talmud.

More important, more than the volumes themselves, the Introductions give me the opportunity to thank the many people who have given me the encouragement, the stories, the comments, and the corrections that have made *FaxHomily, Drasha,* and *Parsha Perspectives* one of the most widely read weekly *divrei* Torah in the world. Most significant, each Introduction gives me the opportunity to express the gratitude and thanks that I must convey to *Hakodosh Boruch Hu* for the opportunity to spread Torah messages on such a massive scale. May He grant me the strength to continue writing, and the proper vision to put the right words on paper — fax, electronic, newsprint, or otherwise — for many years to come.

Perplexing Parables

One of the dilemmas I face weekly, especially if I cannot find a story of a *tzaddik* or a righteous person, is whether to use an historical anecdote of a secular figure — be it a noble statesman, a sportsman, or even a rogue villain — to make my point. I was once challenged via e-mail for clarifying a point in the parsha with an actual story of a politician. "Why can't you use a *tzaddik* instead?" inquired the writer, a Harvard University student.

That week, the story I used helped clarify a negative character trait, specifically that of Esav. And so I simply answered the writer, "I can't imagine using a story of the Chofetz Chaim to illustrate obsessive control!"

As a youngster, I had heard stories given as parables, especially from those collected by the Dubno Maggid. They featured kings and princes, paupers and tycoons, artists and craftsmen, wise men and fools. The Maggid's genius transformed the world of the imaginary tavern-keeper and the cruel landlord into relevant applications for our daily Torah living.

I always wondered, "What if that cruel king really existed?" After all, Jewish history did not lack its share of tyrants, landlords, or noblemen! What if the vicious ruler was actually Ivan the Terrible, or the hapless worker who flubbed his performance was really Marv Throneberry? A parable was once told by a speaker to explain how others could totally misperceive one man's masterwork. It was about an artist whose masterpiece was totally misunderstood by the masses who misinterpreted his genius based on their ill-perceived notions. After the speech, I wondered, "How much more powerful would the parable have been if the speaker knew that there actually was an artist, namely Henri Matisse, whose "*Le Bateau*" hung for forty-seven days in the Museum of Modern Art, viewed and admired by 116,000 people who did not notice that it was upside down!"

In this volume, I relate a parable to explain a difficult verse in *Parshas Shmini.* The Talmud in *Pesachim* explains how the Torah, in relating the story of Noach and bringing non-kosher animals into the ark, was careful not to describe those animals in a negative fashion. The Torah does not call them "*traif;*" instead, it refers to them as animals that are "not pure."

Thus, the Talmud points out how careful one must be, even to the extent of using seemingly superfluous language, to speak in a positive light.

However, when the Torah explicates the prohibition of non-kosher foods, it seems to abandon its previous protocol and adapt a diametrically-opposed strategy. It does not classify the pig, the hare, and other non-kosher animals that it tells us not to eat as "those that are non-kosher;" rather, it exclaims to us, "Do not eat them, They are traif!" And so the contradiction is glaring.

The Chofetz Chaim explained this with a parable:

There was once a governor who was a guest in a backward village. Having been served muddy tea, he chided his subjects for using dirty water and taught them water purification and filtering techniques.

The problem was that a week later, while putting out a fire, the villagers let the town burn while they were busy purifying the water for use in extinguishing the flames! "You fools!" shouted the governor. "You purify water when you are at leisure! When a fire burns, you must use the water that will do the job quickly and efficiently — even if it is a little muddy!"

The lesson taught by the Chofetz Chaim clarified the Torah's usage of strict and harsh words in situations fraught with spiritual peril, as opposed to a more refined expression used in relating a narrative.

And then I thought, how much more powerful would the parable be if it really happened! And then I read that it did! Well, sort of.

In 1863, during the height of the Civil War, President Abraham Lincoln inspected a Union fortress, Fort Wood. During his assessment, Confederate troops began firing on the fort, making Lincoln the only sitting President to be shot at in the course of a war.

A young soldier named Oliver Wendell Holmes, who would one day become a Justice of the United States Supreme Court, saw the President being shot at, his tall frame protruding over the ramparts of the fortification.

"You idiot!" he shouted. "They are shooting at us! Get down!"

There it was, the Chofetz Chaim's parable, straight out of history.

And so I began looking at the world through different eyes — eyes that try to learn something about life not only from the Chumash and Talmud, but eyes that learn from the street peddlers of Manhattan to the promise peddlers of Washington.

I do not write this book necessarily to wring moral lessons from the subjects contained within; rather, I use the real-life figures and their antics to portray human characteristics that I intend to discuss. Some traits are honorable; some are ignoble. But as easily as the Torah teaches us how to behave, from the tales of its towering figures (the forefathers, the prophets, and sages) it also tells us how not to act, using the stories of Esav, Og, Dasan, and Aviram. The nature of humans does not change, only the depth of their actions.

I remember my revered *Rebbe*, Reb Mendel Kaplan, of blessed memory, commenting on a conversation that a few of us were having during a period in the Carter administration. The President was pressuring Israel for certain concessions, surely a heinous act in the eyes of 16-year-old statesmen!

"He's a real *rasha,*" shouted one of the boys.

"Yeah," shouted another, "He's the worst President we ever had for Israel!"

Reb Mendel stopped us. Though he did not offer his opinion on the political machinations of the administration, he laughed. "*Rasha*?" he reacted incredulously. "In Europe we knew what a real *rasha* was. In America we don't have *r'sha'im.* We have babies!"

It is surely difficult to make inter-generational analogies, even harder to create comparisons from Torah personalities to modern-day figures. Nevertheless, using a real individual to portray a character trait also displayed in a Torah personality in no way makes the subjects perfectly analogous. One may be a real *rasha,* the other just a baby.

The parables or anecdotes are there to make us think that in some way or another a kernel of the character lies dormant thorough history.

Preachers and theologians are wont to compare Biblical personalities directly with world leaders, or calamities past with mishaps present. Torah *hashkafa* has a differing view.

The Mishna tells us, "If the forebears are angelic, then we are human. And if the forebears are only human, then we are like donkeys!" (*Shabbos* 112b)

We like to consider ourselves human. Surely, we must visualize our predecessors in generations past— and infinitesimally more so in Biblical times — as superhuman.

Therefore, we must conclude that their transgressions are not our transgressions, and their virtues are not ours as well. Abraham's loyalty, kindness, and compassion are the foundations of every Jewish act of hospitality and kindness that followed for generations to come. Moshe's humility is the standard-bearer for all generations, an incomparable level we all must aspire to attain. And when we realize the veracity of the adage, "If the forebears were angels, then we are mere mortals; and if they were mere mortals, then we are only donkeys," we know the best we can do is try.

Unfortunately, small-minded writers equate present-day moral dilemmas of a simple nature with those carrying the enormous issues of the Torah. Comparing strife in the home or dysfunction in the family with the turmoil surrounding Biblical figures is ludicrous! Opportunistic newsmen compare post-office massacres with the Holocaust. And small-minded preachers equate at-risk teens to images of Ishmael and Esav. Those analogies are as simple as comparing the flight of a bumblebee to the flight of a 747. Yes, they both are guided by a set of physical properties, governed by the laws of physics and aerodynamics. Yes, they both fly. But they are two totally different forms of flight — each with its own unique qualities. The analogies of the bumblebee to the plane must be used to understand aerodynamic theory. So, too, the stories of the Torah must be used to teach us proper moralistic and Torah behavior. Then we can springboard to our own lives without ever diminishing the greatness of our *Avos* by comparing theirs to our own.

People often get carried away with superlatives; they become emotionally charged by incidents and make the most inane comparisons.

I'm reminded about an incident George Stephanopolous, President Clinton's neophyte aide and confidant during his first administration, relates in his book *All Too Human*. The President was about to deliver the State of the Union address to Congress. The wrong speech was accidentally downloaded into the teleprompter! Imagine, the President was about to have delivered a speech intended for the Ladies Auxiliary Association of the National Audubon Society to both houses of Congress!

Stephanopolous burst into the audio-visual room, which contained the errant computer that had switched the files, screaming, "This is the worst thing that has ever happened!"

An aide named Feldman corrected the problem with the flick of a small switch and shrugged. "The Holocaust was pretty bad too," he countered.

I would venture to say that in the worlds of Jewish theology and history until the epoch of *Moshiach,* we have experienced all the wonderful superlatives.

We have seen the greatest; we were taught by the brightest; we experienced the kindest; we were led by the humblest; and we witnessed the most glorious. I hope and pray that the terrible superlatives of our recent history, will never, ever, be surpassed in this world, and the wonderful superlatives of our ancient heritage will only be bested through the one anointed.

Our journey in this world, meanwhile, is the quest for greatness in a world of mediocrity. We set our sights on the mountains of our past, hoping to climb high enough to say, "I was there."

For though we are not, or never will be, Avrahams or Moshes, or even Ba'al Shem Tovs or Vilna Gaons, we can translate what they have done and apply it, on our level, to our lives. We do not have to compare our actions directly to those of Moshe's, or to any of our holy ancestors, but rather we must evaluate our wills and desires to the lessons we learn from our patriarchal and matriarchal predecessors.

Life is filled with comparisons. And so the parables of reality cast the historical relevance of incidents into a perspective for our future. As art does more than imitate life by defining it, a parable or an anecdote is only there to get people thinking — not to diminish the base subject.

We did not need an Einstein to give us the laws of social and moral relativity. We learn from everybody, every incident, and every thing. We are constantly influenced by our surroundings. Our job is to carry out the function of the kidneys and filter the impurities from the worlds that we ingest.

Perfect Parables?

Does everything have a perfect parable? Of course not. But to wet the palate, and try to make difficult concepts easier to swallow, I try.

I am reminded how the Kovno Jew explained the concept of wireless radio to his friend.

The fellow asked his friend, "How does this wireless radio work?"

The friend responded. "Imagine you have this great big dog, and its head is in Vilna, and its tail is in Kovno. You pull the tail in Kovno, and it barks in Vilna!"

"Right!" said the friend.

"Well," continued the first fellow, "wireless is the same thing, only without the dog!"

Is it a perfect explanation? Of course not, but I guess simple minds are simply amused. And so I try. For others, and hopefully myself as well, I hope I've lent some substantial meaning to the mysteries of mundane life as well as to its essential eternals.

So when my tales (pardon the pun) are not perfectly analogous, which is every so often, I hope the point is well taken. And if they don't exude inspiration, perhaps they can bring a smile to the lips and a chuckle to the soul.

Once again, I express my deep gratitude to all those who have provided me with the Torah knowledge and insight which has been incorporated into my life as well as this volume.

Foremost, I thank a patron of the *Parsha Parables* series as well as many other innovative projects that have enhanced awareness of *midos* and *maasim tovim*, Avraham Berkowitz, who, through *Keren Ma'asim Tovim* has assured the production of the Parsha Parables series. His advice and guidance have been as endearing as his personal friendship. May he and his wife, Mindy, see much *nachas* from their entire family.

Yehuda and Beth Honig have been wonderful friends for many years. Prominent *ba'alei chessed* in our community, their dedication in memory of Zoltan Honig, of blessed memory, has ensured that this edition of *Parsha Parables*, will enhance the homes of thousands of readers, and benefit the Yeshiva of South Shore as well. May they enjoy much *nachas* from all their children and see much *hatzlacha* from all their endeavors.

I thank my good friend and long time *chavrusa,* Howard (Moshe Zvi) Birnbaum, for the initial inspiration to turn the faxes into books, and the friendship and support he has shown from the very first day we met. May he and his wife Sora see much health, happiness and *nachas* from all their wonderful deeds.

I am grateful to the Hirsch and Friedman families who through the Henry and Myrtle Hirsch Foundation are prime sponsors of *FaxHomily.* They have been a crucial conduit for the dissemination of my weekly column to nearly 14,000 subscribers.

I thank my friend, and advisor on electronic media, Rabbi Yaakov Menken of torah.org, for making sure that, from St. Petersburg to Pittsburgh, the subscribers receive their weekly *Drasha.* I envy his eternal reward for the role he plays in delivering so much Torah, to so many people, and to so many places throughout the world.

My friend and enduring editor Abby Mendelson has taken time from other projects that are read by multitudes to focus on my little *bubeh ma'asehs,* both in his editing of my weekly essays and the major amount of time he devoted to this work. His cosmopolitan appointments, always carrying a passport of Torah, have broadened my horizons and thus expanded the appeal of the *Parsha Parables* series.

Ethel Gottlieb has been a wonderful copy editor, checking on references, nuances, and accuracy. Hailing from rabbinic roots, her expertise has sprouted fruit that thousands of readers enjoy.

I express gratitude to those who read and commented on this manuscript as well as the weekly faxes, among them Rabbi Yitzchok Wolpin, Rabbi Yaakov Reisman, Rabbi Moshe Weinberger, Dr. Steven Kollander, and my cousin Rabbi Sholom Kamenetsky.

From theory to practical application, there are many highways and byways one must travel. I thank all of those who took this book one step closer to your home.

There is Paula Tausch, for the administration of the entire publishing process; Dena Peker, of Dynagrafik, who typeset this work; Gershon Eichorn, of Spotlight Design, who designed the cover; Feivel Weinreich, of Noble Book Press, who printed it; Yitzchok Feldheim, of Feldheim Publishers, who distributed it, Neil Rosen, who warehoused it; all the bookstores that carried it; and, of course, you, who bought it!

My dear wife Sora is a mirror that is able to show me who I really am without telling me. Like the mirror's subtle message that prevents one from walking outside with hair unkempt or buttons missing their marks, in her amazingly delicate way she helps me fix gaffes and fine-tune stories before they leave the keyboard. She also makes sure I don't leave the house *sans* buttons as well!

Though, this introduction deals with my thanks *vis-à-vis* this work, I would be remiss not to thank her for also fine tuning every aspect of my life and the life of our children. Our family plays a harmonious tune that I pray is sweet music to Hashem, and she is the conductor of that magnificent symphony.

I thank my children, who must bear with me when I turn our mundane trips into next week's parables. Window washers perched atop skyscrapers become those who have the ability to look straight ahead and see their human peers as large and important as themselves, or look down and see their fellows humans as tiny insects. Subway conductors become national leaders who determine the fate of their passengers with the flick of tiny switches. Even trips to the park become springboards for parabolic reflection. I thank them for bearing with me as I convert the simple joys of their childhood into philosophical treatises.

My parents and in-laws have been a source of strength and encouragement and ideas. May Hashem give my father the strength to build Torah institutions in which Jewish children grow to become the parables of proper Torah life — shining examples who make this world a brighter place. May Hashem give my mother the strength to continue to be a foundation of support for generations of children and grandchildren who strive to emulate the forebears of our illustrious ancestry.

My brother and sisters, as well as brothers-in-law and sisters-in-law, all share in this work.

I especially thank Rabbi Pinchos Lipschutz, publisher of *Yated Ne'eman*, who has been a great source of inspiration and advice for many years. May he continue spreading only good news throughout the world.

As has become my custom, I'd like to end my Introduction with a story:

As England's Foreign Secretary, Lord Balfour was supposed to deliver a major address at a Texas ceremony that went on and on and on. Last on the program, he knew that he had already lost a major portion of his audience. And so when the master of ceremonies called him to come forward and give his address, he simply stated. "My dear friends. For three hours, you have been hearing speech after speech. Now I am asked to give you my address — which I will: 10 Carllton Gardens, London, England." With that he left the podium.

My dear reader, I have written a long-enough Introduction. I'd love to hear from you as well! *My* address is on the front page of this book. Read, enjoy, and write!

Mordechai Kamenetzky
Woodmere, NY
Elul, 5760

ספר בראשית

The Book of Genesis

PARSHAS BRAISHIS

Dealing with the Enemy

Of the few verses in the Torah that define man's evil inclination, the *yetzer hara,* many appear in *Sefer Braishis.* After all, if Hashem created man with a *yetzer hara,* then that man ought to know a bit more about the evil inclination — and be provided with a formula to defeat it.

Indeed, the *yetzer hara* struck early and often in *Genesis,* first when Adam and Chava sinned by eating from the Tree of Knowledge, later when Kayin offered an inferior sacrifice — then slew his brother Hevel in a fit of jealous anger. At that last instance, Hashem revealed to mankind the nature of the beast.

"Surely," Hashem told Kayin, "if you improve you can carry him (i.e., the *yetzer hara*); and if you do not improve then he crouches at your door and [directs] his desire is toward you. But you can rule over him!" (*Genesis 4:7*)

Clearly, it is odd that Hashem seemed to mitigate the severity of the danger. He did not end the warning with the words, "if you do not improve, he (the *yetzer hara*) crouches at your door, and his desire is toward you, and he will defeat you." Instead, Hashem said that if one does not improve, then the *yetzer hara* crouches at his door with intent to harm. But then, in an anticlimactic final warning, Hashem left us with these words of encouragement: "But you will rule over him!"

What kind of warning is that? Shouldn't the admonition have stated, "and if you do not improve, he crouches at your door, his desire is toward you, and he will rule over you?"

There was an itinerant Jew, who, while visiting the town of Radin, in Poland, had earned a reputation

as a thief. In truth, the man had stolen from many people — including those who had hosted him as a guest in their homes. After a short time, the carpetbagger was clearly identified, and the community was duly warned, so that the next time he came to Radin they would not invite him into their homes.

Of course, the townsfolk heeded the warnings, and the next time the man came he received not one invitation — except from the Radiner *Rosh Yeshiva,* Rabbi Naftali Trop.

Upon hearing of his offer of hospitality, some of the prominent members of the community approached Reb Naftali. "The man you invited is a thief!" they exclaimed. "Last time he was here, he walked off with some of his host's valuables. You mustn't let him sleep in your home!"

Yet Reb Naftali was not phased. "The Torah tells us that a thief must pay a fine for his actions," he said. "It does not tell us that a thief should not be invited to eat or sleep. I have a responsibility to invite guests. If I am afraid that they may steal, well, that's my problem. I guess I must make sure that all my valuables are guarded. However, those fears can in no way relieve me of my responsibility to shelter my fellow Jews. I have two issues to deal with, and one should not interfere with the other!"

The Torah's message to Kayin is twofold — signaling two approaches to battling the *yetzer hara*. First, you can get the *yetzer hara* out of your way completely: "you can carry him." That is, you can place him out of your path and lift him out of your sight. However, that method may not work for all of us. Those who cannot rise to that level still have the *yetzer hara* crouching in their doorways — even sleeping over as a houseguest! Though he is lying in ambush, we cannot ignore him — and we cannot give up hope. Instead, we must deal with him, if not directly then through subterfuge. For example, if you have a tendency to become exasperated, you might try channeling your frustration against evil. If you are improperly stingy, then you might try unnecessary shopping splurges as a curative. A lack of faith may be channeled to helping those in need — even if you don't assure them that Hashem will provide!

Throughout, the Torah is telling us that when the *yetzer hara* is part of our lives we must deal with him. We can never use the excuse of saying that the desire was too great and therefore insurmountable. So if we let him in the door we have to make sure that we are able to fulfill the *mitzvos* in spite of his presence.

If you tame the beast correctly, he may crouch and wait for you. But you will rule over him. And you will learn to use his resources for your benefit.

Parshas Noach

The Rain Maker

Noach lived through trying times, to say the least. He survived not only a generation of spiritual chaos, but endured the world's physical annihilation as well. However, Hashem walked with him and guided him, instructing Noach every step of the way. Warning Noach of the impending flood, He instructed him to build an ark and bring all the animals to it. Yet for all of his efforts, Noach was labeled as a man who lacked faith. The Torah tells us that, "Noach, with his wife and sons and his son's wives with him, went into the ark because of the waters of the Flood" (*Genesis 7:7*).

The classic Torah commentator, Rashi quotes a *Midrash* proclaiming that Noach did lack faith — if only to a small degree — since he entered the ark only "because of the waters of the Flood." The clear implication is that Noach did not enter the ark until the rain forced him to do so.

The obvious question is how can we say that Noach lacked faith — even to a tiny extent? He had to believe! After all, he spoke to Hashem! He built the ark! He gathered all the animals! He was the only person in his generation to understand — and be concerned about — the impending doom! Surely, he — of all people —must have believed! It is inconceivable to think otherwise. So why is there a complaint against Noach? What is wrong with waiting to enter until he has no choice? To what possible degree is he considered lacking in faith?

Rabbi Shimshon Sherer, Rav of Congregation Kehilas Zichron Mordechai, tells the following story.

A small town was experiencing a severe drought. While the community synagogues each prayed separately for rain, there was no relief. Both tears and prayers failed to unlock the sealed heavens, and for months no rains came.

Finally, the town's eldest sage called a meeting with prominent community rabbis and lay leaders. "There are two items lacking in our approach," he said, "faith and unity. Each one of you must impress upon your congregation the need to believe. If we are united and sincere, our prayers will be answered!"

Then the sage declared that all the synagogues in the city would join together for a day of *tefilah*. Everyone — men, women, and children — would join together for this event. "I assure you," he exclaimed, "that if we meet both criteria — faith and unity — no one will leave that prayer service without getting drenched!"

Since there was no *shul* large enough to contain the entire community, the date was set to gather and *daven* in a field! For the next few weeks, all the rabbis spoke about *bitachon* and *achdus* (faith and unity). Finally, on the designated day the entire town gathered in a large field whose crops had long ago withered from the severe drought. Men, women, and children all came together and anxiously waited for the venerable sage to begin the service.

As the elderly rabbi walked up to the podium, his eyes scanned the enormous crowd that had filled the large field and then dimmed in dismay. The rabbi began shaking his head in dissatisfaction. "This will never work," he moaned dejectedly. "The rain will not come." Slowly he left the podium.

The other rabbis on the dais were shocked. "But *rebbe*," they pleaded, "everyone is here — and we are all united! Surely, everyone must believe that the rains will fall! Otherwise, no one would have bothered to come on a working day!"

The rabbi shook his head slowly and sadly.

"No," he said. "They don't really believe. I scanned the entire crowd. Nobody even brought a raincoat!"

The Torah demands a much greater level of faith from Noach — much more than he demonstrated. Before the fact, Noach's instinctive faith should have kicked in, turning what may have appeared to him as a bright sunny day into one filled with fatal flood water. But he waited to see if the rains would really come. Instead, he should have bolted into the ark the morning that the Flood was set to arrive. Indeed, even at the storm's first moments he seemed to ignore its impending ferocity. He waited, lingering until the torrents forced him into the ark — almost like someone who hears predictions of a tornado and stands outside waiting for the funnel cloud to knock at his door! The truth is that that at zero hour Noach should have moved himself and his family into the ark — regardless of what was in the sky. And for not doing that he was chided — because true faith requires true action. And action reigns supreme — even during the driest periods of world history.

Parshas Lech Lecha

Wake Up Call

Hashem has different ways in which He revealed Himself to mortal men. The Torah, for example, tells us that Moshe was special, for the revelations he experienced are described with the expression "face-to-face." Others, however, saw Hashem only in a vision. In this *parsha,* the Torah tells us of Avram's very animated vision. "And the word of Hashem came to Avram in a vision, 'Fear not, Avram'... and He took Avram outside and said, 'Count the stars, if you are able to count them...Thus shall be your offspring" (*Genesis 15:1-5*).

Avram went outside and tried to count the stars. Then he went back inside, and the Torah tells us about the *Bris Bain Ha'besarim* — the frightening vision of the Covenant Between the Parts: "The sun set, and a deep sleep fell upon Avram. And behold, a dark fear descended upon him" *(Genesis 15:12).*

It is interesting to contrast the two visions. The first seems dynamic and upbeat, while the second has a sense of doom. Commentaries explain that the first vision engenders the good news about the growth and future prosperity of Avram's descendants, while the second vision predicts the Jewish people's exile in Egypt — causing Avram alarm. But a deeper look at the verses indicates that Avram trembled as a "a dark fear descended upon him," i.e., before he heard the news about the Egyptian bondage. In fact, the fear set in as soon as the deep slumber fell upon him. Could the sleep alone precipitate the fear? Perhaps the deep slumber set off some impending feeling of doom. If so, how?

During the 1940s, Rabbi Shimshon Zelig Fortman was the Rav of Congregation Knesseth Israel in Far Rockaway. During that period, naysayers had all but discounted any chance of a rebirth of Orthodox Jewry. Indeed, Orthodox Jews hardly had a voice in government, they were disorganized and fragmented, and, with the complete destruction of European Jewry, traditional Torah *Yiddishkeit* seemed clearly a thing of the past.

Yet, not everyone believed those dire predictions to be true. Indeed, Rabbi Fortman had a young son-in-law, Moshe, who had studied in Yeshiva Ner Israel in Baltimore. With great regularity, the young man would tell his father-in-law how he saw a future for Orthodox Jewry that was filled with honor and power. Their representatives would have direct access to Congress, the Senate, and even the President of the United States. They would influence legislation with their values and fill stadiums with Torah assemblies and prayer gatherings!

Although he greatly admired his son-in-law, Rabbi Fortman was very concerned about the young man's unrealistic dreams, feeling that they would distract him and prevent him from ever accomplishing anything of note. At the time, Rabbi Yosef Kahaneman, the Ponovezer Rav, had recently come to America to raise funds for his yeshiva in Israel and was staying with Rabbi Fortman. Rabbi Fortman asked his guest, himself a Holocaust survivor and rebuilder of Torah in Israel, to have a talk with his son-in-law. Surely, Rabbi Fortman thought, Rabbi Kahaneman would terminate Moshe's fantasies and teach him a valuable lesson about the realities of accomplishment.

But Rabbi Kahaneman had ideas of his own. When Moshe and Rabbi Kahaneman met, the Rav listened intently for nearly an hour, then told young Moshe, "Dream my son. Continue to dream.

In fact, you can continue to dream as long as you live. But remember one thing — don't ever fall asleep!"

Young Moshe didn't. In fact, he went on to build a great Torah career — and was eventually known to hundreds of thousands of Jews the world over, respected by kings and presidents, and honored by the United States Senate. Indeed, he was a man who may well have been one of the most influential personalities in the contemporary emergence of Torah Jewry. No, Moshe did not sleep; instead, he was known and cherished as Rabbi Moshe Sherer, the President of Agudath Israel of America.

Perhaps, homiletically speaking, Avram began to tremble the moment that sleep commenced because he understood that visions of greatness may occur. He knew that his children will number the multitude of stars that he was not able to count! But when darkness fell, and Avram drifted into a deep sleep, he shuddered. Because nothing good could appear if he fell completely asleep! For when the visionary sleeps, all his dreams are lost in slumber!

Parshas Vayeira

The Life of the Party

"Was that some party!" Those words, often slurred, generally pronounced as revelers teeter from the exquisite ballrooms of posh hotels and banquet halls, fail to capture the essence of what truly makes a party great. Well, what really does make a great party? Caterers will insist it's the food. Musicians claim it's the music and dancing. And, of course, florists will tell you it's the décor. In this *parsha*, however, Rashi tells us it is absolutely something else.

The Torah tells us of a party — a great party. Avraham was 100-years-old, and his wife Sora was 90, when Yitzchak was miraculously born. Three years later, when Yitzchak was weaned, they made what the Torah terms "a great party" (*Genesis 21:8*). Which brings us back to our question: what makes a great party? What made that party great? Rashi explains that it was because "the great people of the generation attended: Shem, the son of Noach; Aiver; and Avimelech."

Why does Rashi interpret a great party as one that has great participants? Maybe it was great because it had a 14-piece band? Maybe it was great because it was held in the grand ballroom of the Canaan Hilton? Maybe Sora and Avraham hired the most exclusive caterer? What caused Rashi to explain "great party" as one with great people?

Not so long ago, the Yeshiva of South Shore in Hewlett, New York, hosted its first annual *safrus* exhibition in memory of Alisa Flatow, of blessed memory,

killed by Arab terrorists during a year of study in Israel.

The fair, which highlighted the art of the *sofer*, the Jewish scribe, had an array of remarkable hands-on exhibits. There were tables at which children were taught how to write letters for a Torah using a quill, parchment, and special ink. There was a display that featured how *tefillin* are made, from the hide to the holy finished product. There was even an exhibit where students, aided by Yeshiva teachers, learned the art of tying knots, creating the sacred fringes that transform a four-cornered garment into a *talis katon*. But the highlight of the exhibition was the opportunity to participate in writing an actual Torah to be placed in the Yeshiva's new sanctuary. The children sat with a *sofer* in front of the parchment and participated as the letters turned from words to sentences, converting raw animal skin into the most sacred item on earth.

One 7-year-old, Moshe Daphna, went from table to table, learning the process of making *tefillin*, trying his hand at *safrus* calligraphy, and learning how to make a pair of *tzitzis*. Finally, he had the opportunity to participate, in a small way, in the adventure of a lifetime — writing a letter in the Torah.

The young boy stood in veneration as he pointed to letters and watched the *sofer*, with his practiced hands, transform the drops of ink into beautiful black letters that glistened on the parchment. The boy stood staring at the letter that had just been inscribed for eternity.

Then in all seriousness he turned to the *sofer*. "Rabbi," the young boy began, "this is awesome!" He pondered a moment and finally spoke. "Can I ask you a question?"

"Surely!" the learned scribe smiled, thinking about the historical or *halachic* questions the aspiring *sofer* might propose.

"Good!" the boy beamed. And then in all innocence he proceeded to ask, "Do you do birthday parties?"

We must understand greatness with the innocence and purity of a small boy who is tired of magicians and clowns entertaining at parties. For even a young child knows that there is no greater "great party" than one filled with greatness itself. Because greatness comes not in the form of balloon-filled ballrooms that will burst the aspirations of the participants. Distinction will not develop from Titanic-type dance floors that leave the guests with a sinking feeling. And Judaism will not flourish through hockey-themed Bar Mitzvos that leave children questioning the true goals of life.

Rashi understands the words "great party" with a Torah vision of greatness. Great parties enlighten and inspire through their participants. Great celebrations glorify the greatness of the Creator through the blessings He bestows upon His humble revelers.

You can have a wild party with wild activities. And you can have a raucous party with blaring music. But in order to have a great party you need great guests.

Parshas Chayai Sora

Soul Trustee

How often do we cancel plans or change a course of action on the say-so of the weatherman — but plan our activities in contrast with the predictions of the Torah? Even Noach, who built the ark under intense pressure, was held accountable for his lack of instinctive faith. And on that level of faith, unfortunately, all of us are a little wet behind the ears.

When Avraham sought a wife for his son Yitzchak, he called no one other than his trusted loyal servant, Eliezer. Eliezer, was one of the primary soldiers who aided Avraham during his battle to rescue Lot. In fact, until Hashem informed Avraham of the forthcoming birth of Yitzchak, Eliezer was considered to be Avraham's heir apparent. Nicknamed *Damesek,* meaning one who draws from the wellsprings of his master, the devoted Eliezer was Avraham's right-hand-man.

Yet, before sending him, the Torah informs us that "Avraham told Eliezer, the elder of Avraham's household, who was in complete charge of every one of Avraham's possessions, to swear that he would not take a girl from Canaan for Yitzchak. Eliezer swore in the name of Hashem, the Master of the heaven and the earth " (*Genesis 24:2-3*).

So did Avraham instruct his most trusted aide to get the proper soul mate for Yitzchak. Eliezer was to go back to Avraham's hometown and find a girl from the right family, raised in the proper environment. In addition, Avraham warned Eliezer that Yitzchak was not to leave Canaan. Indeed, his charge was forceful: he used strong language and made his trusted servant swear. "Be careful — watch out! Lest you bring my son there!" (*Genesis 24:6*).

Yet in this context the Torah's reiteration of Eliezer's domestic position is perplexing. Isn't the juxtaposition — glorifying Eliezer's position as "the elder of his household, who was in complete charge of every one of Avraham's possessions" — contradictory with the severe scrutiny and pressure that Avraham placed on him in reference to Yitzchak's matrimonial requirements? If Avraham trusted Eliezer with his entire worldly possessions, why did he make him swear in this instance? And if Eliezer had to swear in regard to Yitzchak, then why was he defined, in the very verse that displayed Avraham's suspicion, as "the elder of his household, who was in complete charge of every one of Avraham's possessions?" Isn't the fact that Eliezer had to swear obvious evidence that he, in fact, was not in charge?

Rabbi Yisrael Lipkin of Salant, the founder of the *mussar* movement, once stayed at an inn. That night, the inn became quite crowded, and the innkeeper realized that he was low on meat. Seeing a distinguished and pious-looking Jew with a beard, the innkeeper approached Reb Yisrael. "Are you perhaps a *shochet* (ritual slaughterer)?" the innkeeper asked. "You see, I am running low on meat, and I must slaughter one of the cows that I have in the barn." Reb Yisrael was taken aback. "I would love to help," he stammered, "but unfortunately I am not a *shochet*."

The next morning Rabbi Lipkin approached the innkeeper. "I have a great business opportunity," he said. "If you were to invest a few hundred rubles with me, I can guarantee you a nice return."

The innkeeper looked quizzically at the rabbi. "Reb Yid," he said, "I hardly know you! How do you expect me to invest with you? Give me a few references, and as many days, and let me check out the deal in its entirety. Then we can meet and I'll make my decision."

"Aha!" the great *Mussar* luminary exclaimed. "Just yesterday, you were about to trust me with the ritual

slaughter of your cow. Based on my countenance, and my frock and beard, you were going to feed your guests with that meat. Nevertheless, you would not invest a few rubles on those same grounds. Shouldn't one treat his spiritual resolutions with the same level of suspicion as his financial ones?"

The *Be'er Mayim Chayim* explains: in the context of Avraham's admonitions, the Torah specifically reiterates that Eliezer "was the elder of Avraham's household, who was in complete charge of every one of Avraham's possessions."

For buying stocks and bonds, investing in real estate, or even purchasing appliances or furniture, Eliezer had free reign. Yet when it came to Yitzchak's future, that high status was not enough. Avraham made Eliezer swear in the name of Hashem that he would bring a suitable wife for Yitzchak.

Avraham's spiritual concerns were by no means on the same level as those he had for his mundane needs. Though Eliezer was in complete charge of every one of Avraham's material possessions, when it came to Avraham's *spiritual* future, even Eliezer was suspect. For when determining one's spiritual needs, a sole trustee is not necessarily a soul trustee.

PARSHAS TOLDOS

With Death Do Us Part

After a debilitating stroke, Rabbi Chaim Shmuelevitz, the Rosh Yeshiva of the Mirrer Yeshiva in Jerusalem, continued to deliver a weekly *mussar shmues* (ethical sermon) at the yeshiva. Hundreds of students strained to hear his brilliant words of wisdom that were peppered with anecdotes and aphorisms shedding new light on the age-old words of the sages of yore. But one day, discussing *Parshas Toldos*, the Rosh Yeshiva stunned his audience with his opening remarks.

"*Ich gai shtarben*! (I am going to die!)" he announced. Then, in a raspy voice, he repeated the words over and over again. "*Ich gai shtarben*!" The students' faces turned ashen. They were not sure whether or not to summon ambulances and medical teams when he suddenly stopped, smiled, and finished his thought, "that is exactly what Esav told his brother Yaakov in this portion!"

Indeed, the transaction in which Esav gave up his birthright for a bowl of lentil soup was preceded by those very words. "Behold, I am going to die," Esav cried, "so why do I need my birthright?" (*Genesis* 25:32)

The thought of death was clearly a catalyst in Esav's decision to rid himself of the birthright and its responsibilities. But why? Everyone dies. However, what did Esav's premonition of the ultimate end have to do with his decision to trade the birthright for lentil soup? Could Esav not just as easily have responded to Yaakov's offer in the following manner: "Behold, the birthright carries too much responsibility. What do I need it for?" What does the concept of death have to do with it?

In the summer of 1976, a student of the Telshe Yeshiva related the following story. An airplane carrying a Telshe student back to Cleveland began experiencing severe turbulence. The young man became quite nervous, but, after seeing that his own *Rosh Yeshiva,* Rabbi Mordechai Gifter, was sitting in front of him, he felt more secure. "After all," the young man thought, "with such a *tzaddik* (righteous man) on board, what possibly could go wrong?"

Suddenly the captain's voice came over the intercom. "We are experiencing some difficulty with the plane's hydraulic system," he said, "and may be forced to make an emergency landing. Everyone please return to your seat, fasten your seatbelt, and follow the instructions given by your flight attendants."

The young man quickly leaned forward toward his Rebbe. "Perhaps we are in danger," he said. "I have a *Tehillim* in my carry-on luggage. Are there any particular Psalms or prayers I should recite?"

Rav Gifter reassured the young man and suggested a few appropriate Psalms. Then he urged him to buckle up and prepare for landing. The Torah sage's advice was interrupted by shouts coming from a frantic passenger sitting next to the student.

"Stewardess," the distraught man bellowed, "quick! Get over here! Make me a double Scotch on the rocks. See if you can make it the best — Johnny Walker Blue Label! Better make it fast, and better make it good, 'cause it may be my last drink before I die!"

The Chofetz Chaim, Rabbi Yisrael Meir Kagan of Radin, explains the Mishnah in *Pirkei Avos* that tells us to "repent one day before our death" (*Avos 2:15*). Obviously, those of us who do not know when that day will arrive must reflect and ask forgiveness daily. But the catalyst of serious reflection and sobriety is the very thought of the final moment — death. Its approach should shake us — if not wake us — into *teshuvah*. Indeed, the fear of death should instill the fear of the ultimate Judge and His final reckoning.

Esav's approach, however, was disturbingly different. "I will cast away any vestige of responsibility or spirituality, because, after all, tomorrow I may die." The source of his attitude of flippant Epicureanism is the very one that prompts our own religious anxiety.

And so, for a bowl of lentil soup, a craved-for cocktail gulped down in a moment of fear, Esav abandoned his world of eternity. The motivating factor behind his *faux pas* should have inspired him to seek the meaning of life. Instead, death was his motivation for a demeaning desire. For us, on the other hand, it should motivate to desire meaning.

Parshas Vayeitzei

Brothers in Scorn

Yaakov's first encounter with his future wife Rochel was significant, encompassing varied emotions, each of which merits lengthy discussion. Upon greeting her at a well, Yaakov feeds her sheep, kisses her, cries, and then identifies himself as the brother of her father (*Genesis 29:10-12*).

Such designation needs explanation. Yaakov was not a brother of Rochel's father Lavan: instead, he was a nephew, the son of Lavan's sister, Rivka. Why then did Yaakov refer to himself as a brother of Lavan? The Talmudic tractate of *Megilah* explains that Lavan's notorious reputation preceded him. He was nicknamed *Lavan HaArami*, or Lavan the charlatan. He was known not only to be avaricious but to be unscrupulous as well. So Yaakov wanted to lay the ground rules with his future bride. "If your father will act in a conniving way, then I am his brother in trickery. However, if he will act honorably, then I will respond in kind."

What needs clarification, however, is why begin a marital relationship on such a note? What precedent is Yaakov setting with such a powerful declaration?

Rabbi Meir Shapiro was a leader of Polish Jewry in the years before World War II. In addition to being the chief Rabbi of Lublin; building and maintaining one of the world's largest and most beautiful yeshivos, Yeshivas Chachmei Lublin; he was also one of the first Orthodox members of the Polish parliament, the Sejm. A courageous leader, Rabbi Shapiro's vision

and unwavering commitment to Torah values gained him the respect of Jews and gentiles alike.

During his first weeks as the leader of the Orthodox Jewish delegation, Rabbi Shapiro was approached by a Polish parliamentary deputy, Professor Lutoslawski, a known anti-Semite whose devious legislation constantly deprived minorities of their civil and economic rights.

Standing in front of a group of parliamentarians in the halls of the Sejm, the depraved deputy began, "Rabbi," he shouted, a sly smile spreading across his evil face, "I have a wonderful new way for Jews to make a living. They can skin dead dogs."

Without missing a beat, Rabbi Shapiro shot back. "Impossible, their representatives would never allow it."

The Professor looked puzzled. "Whose representatives? The Jews'?"

"No," smiled Rav Meir, "the dog deputies."

Flustered, the vicious bigot tried once more. "Well, my dear Rabbi," he continued sarcastically, "Do you know that on the entrance gate to the city of Schlesien there is an inscription, 'to Jews and dogs entrance forbidden?'"

Rabbi Meir just shrugged his shoulders, "I guess we will never be able to visit that city together."

Needless to say, nary an anti-Semitic word was ever pointed in Rabbi Meir's direction again.

Yaakov knew that to initiate his destiny in the confines of a hostile environment he should proclaim the rules loudly and clearly. He would not allow himself to be swayed, duped, or connived by anyone, even the master of deception and ridicule, Lavan the charlatan. In forging the household that would be the basis for a Jewish eternity, Yaakov had to make it clear to his future bride that he, too, could play hardball. In so doing, he sent a message of pride and awareness to his descendants.

Though this Jew who sat in the tent would enter his new environment with brotherly love, if he needed to, he could just as well be a brother in scorn.

PARSHAS VAYISHLACH

Animal House

"Hutz 'n' plutz." That was a fictitious name my mother would give to a place where everything was bliss and things were very simple. It was the home of Chaim Yankel — or whoever was the mythical Jewish character of any given fable. But, believe it or not, there was a place called "Huts 'n' plutz." Of course, the "'n plutz" suffix was not added, nor was the place actually called Huts in the English language. It did, however, take the name in Hebrew. And it was called *Sukkos*. And *Sukkos* are huts.

After Yaakov departed peacefully from his brother, he dwelled in a place for 18 months. When he arrived he built a quasi-infrastructure — homes for his kin and *sukkos*, huts, for his great herd. Then he named the city. He did not call it for the homes he built, rather for the myriad structures that he built for the animals — *Sukkos*. Huts.

Many commentators are puzzled as to why Yaakov chose a name representing the temporary animal structures rather than calling the city Houses, or *Batim*, referring to the more permanent dwellings he erected for his family. After all, is it not more appropriate to name a village after the human abodes than the animal ones? Some answer that naming the city *Sukkos* was a symbolic expression of the paradox of all worldly permanence — and Yaakov was saying that all abodes, from glorious mansions to marble edifices, are only temporal. They are all *Sukkos*. Thus, he named the town *Sukkos*.

My grandfather, Rabbi Yaakov Kamenetzky, of blessed memory, once offered a very practical answer to the question. After

Yaakov constructed homes for both his children and livestock, the dominant feature of the landscape was myriad huts scattered across the countryside. Gazing at the amazingly transformed desert, he appropriately named the town after the way it looked. He called it Huts.

But why does it matter how it looked — or what he called it? Perhaps both questions can be answered as one.

In the northern part of Israel, Yeshiva K'far Chasidim had established itself as a prominent center of Torah scholarship. Students flocked to the Yeshiva to gain spiritual nourishment from the *Mashgiach* (Dean of Ethics), the justly famed Reb Elya Lopian. But the Yeshiva attracted more than students seeking spiritual nourishment.

The basement in which the pasta, flour, and other dry goods were stored also attracted those seeking physical nourishment. It had become infested with rodents! To the problem of a diminishing food supply and nascent health hazard, the students decided on a simple solution: they scoured the rubbish piles of the city and brought a stray cat back to the campus. Every day it would play in the yard, and each evening they would bring it to the basement where it would earn its keep, receiving room and board simultaneously. Within a few weeks there was not a rodent to be found. But the cat remained. Unfortunately, the boys lapsed in their commitment to its welfare, even forgetting to feed it.

One evening, the cat scratched on the screen door of the aged *Mashgiach* Reb Elya Lopian, who was puzzled by its appearance. Not informed about the extermination stratagem of the student body, he wondered where the cat came from. One of the younger students then explained the problem of the mice and their ingenious solution.

"Are there still mice?" Reb Elya asked.

"No," exclaimed the student, "there hasn't been a rodent in days!" Then he smiled while looking down at the cat and added, "Thanks to this fellow."

"And since there are no mice, what has he been eating?" the *Mashgiach* pursued.

The boy just shrugged. He simply did not know.

"Ah," the Sage sighed. "You have been lax in your responsibility and gratitude. I will show you how to feed a cat."

With that, Reb Elya, a man in his eighties, went into his kitchen, poured milk into a saucer, and placed it down for the hungry feline.

At that moment a young student named Kavinsky captured the moment on film. The picture of the white-bearded Torah giant bending down and feeding a cat is a most popular picture for thousands of youngsters in America and Israel. It has become Reb Elya's proud testament that even God's simplest creatures must be cared for, even by a sage in Israel.

The *Ohr HaChaim* a Sefardic sage who lived in the early part of the 18th Century, offers a brilliant and revolutionary explanation to the peculiar name *Sukkos*. He explains that Yaakov *Avinu* did something unprecedented for that era. Realizing that he would be spending a year and a half in unsheltered terrain, he built a sanctuary for animals! Others would have left them in the cold, caring selfishly for only their own welfare and that of their kin. Yaakov, however, was proud of building huts for his animals, and he expressed that pride in naming the entire city not after the act that any husband and father would do, a labor of love that would be personally enjoyed by members of his family. No, Yaakov did not call the village Levittown or Jacobsville. Instead, he named it after his backbreaking labor in service to his temporal flock.

In calling it *Sukkos*, he gave the place a name that told the world he not only cared for his own flesh and blood, but also that he cared for beings who had no one else to depend upon. In so doing, he set the standard for all time, proclaiming the compassion one must accord to the simplest beings, even a cat.

Parshas Vayeishev

Oh, Baby!

Baby. In the 'sixties it was a term of poetic affection. In the schoolyard, its chant — and a directive that the sparring partner stick its head in a sauce usually reserved for a roast — is a verbal taunt usually invoked by one of two immature adversaries.

But when the Torah refers to someone as a child, or a *na'ar,* it is taken very seriously. Literally, the word *na'ar* means child, but one that is neither an infant nor a mature adolescent. So when applied in those circumstances, scholars analyze and deduce.

When infant Moshe was found in a reed basket floating on the Nile, the Torah tells us that the daughter of Pharaoh heard a *na'ar* crying (*Exodus 2:6*). Rashi comments on the apparent anomaly. After all, since the word *na'ar* is not used for an infant, Rashi explains it by quoting *Midrashic* sources that Moshe had a voice like a mature lad.

In this *parsha,* the term *na'ar* is also used, and superficially it is not complimentary. "Yosef was 17-years-old, and was a shepherd with his brothers by the flock, but he was a *na'ar* with the children of Bilhah and Zilpah, his father's wives" *(Genesis 37:2).* Again the expression *na'ar* raises a flag. The *Midrash* obviously feels that that term should be reserved for children younger than teens. And so the *Midrash* asks, is it fitting to label a 17-year-old a *na'ar*? The answer is that at that age Yosef acted immaturely, dressing his hair and adorning his eyes to look handsome. (On the other hand, Ramban feels that the term *na'ar* would apply to Yosef, as he was youngest of the brothers, except for Benjamin who was a mere infant at the time.)

In response to those opinions, the *Sfas Emes* raises a powerful objection. If the term *na'ar* is out of place for anyone even approaching his late teens, then an earlier verse needs clarification.

In *Parshas Vayeira,* Avraham, together with his sons Yitzchak and Yishmael, and his servant Eliezer, traveled for three days fulfilling Hashem's command to bring his son as an offering on Mount Moriah. As he finally saw the mountain, Avraham knew it was time to conclude the journey alone — with only Yitzchak. So Avraham told Yishmael and Eliezer, "remain here with the donkey, and I and the *na'ar* will go yonder" (*Genesis* 22:5).

Yitzchak was 37-years old at the time, yet not one commentator is troubled that his father calls him a baby! Why?

A distraught man once approached my grandfather, Rabbi Yaakov Kamenetzky, of blessed memory. "I know this may not sound like a major problem," he began, "but my 17-year-old daughter is very upset with me. It has come to a point that she hardly talks to me. It began a few nights ago. My wife and I were at a family wedding when my daughter walked by. I introduced her to some distant relatives by saying, 'This is my baby.'

"I could see that at the moment she became very upset. Moments later she pulled me aside and was crying. 'You still think I'm a baby!' she sobbed. 'I am almost eighteen already, and all you do is call me your baby! Won't I ever be a grown-up in your eyes?' Ever since then she doesn't talk to me."

The man shrugged as he pleaded with the Sage. "I really don't want to make this into a major issue, but I'm not sure how to resolve this. Perhaps the *Rosh Yeshiva* can guide me."

Reb Yaakov put his hand on the man's shoulder. "Do you ever visit Monsey?"

At the time, Reb Yaakov's youngest son Reb Avraham, would travel to Monsey every Wednesday to study Torah with his father.

Reb Yaakov invited the disconcerted father to visit, together with his daughter that very Wednes-

day when his youngest son Reb Avraham would be there.

Reb Yaakov assured him that though he would not discuss the incident, he was confident that by the time the visit was over the matter would be resolved.

The next week the man and his daughter visited Reb Yaakov at his Monsey home. Reb Yaakov invited them into the dining room where they discussed a variety of issues from school work to life in pre-war Europe — everything but the incident at the wedding.

About 20 minutes into the conversation, Reb Avraham walked in, books in hand, ready to study with his revered father. Reb Yaakov greeted him affectionately and then introduced Reb Avraham to his guests.

"This is my baby!" exclaimed the revered sage, as he gave a warm hug to his 50-year-old son.

Needless to say, the impact on the 17-year-old girl changed her perspective on her father's comments. Fifteen minutes later they left the house with a renewed and invigorated relationship!

The *Sfas Emes* answers his question very simply. When the Torah in a narrative describes someone as a *na'ar* it is a point of concern, needing explanation, whether complimentary or otherwise. But when a father calls a child his *na'ar* there is no need to explain. It is simple and more than acceptable. And Hashem Himself refers to His children that way. "When Israel was a *na'ar* and I loved him, and since Egypt I have called him My child" *(Hosea 11:1).*

Parshas Miketz

Stuck on Gum

This *parsha* entails the fascinating story of Yosef's rise to power. After interpreting Pharaoh's dream, he was appointed viceroy to Egypt, a land with an impending famine. And Yosef's visionary economic and agricultural solutions ensured that nation's financial and agricultural stability during the ensuing crisis. Indeed, so bad were the times that thousands of Middle Eastern citizens flocked to Egypt to purchase food from him. Among them were the very ones who sold Yosef — his brothers. In a familiar story, Yosef accused them of spying, detained Shimon as a hostage, and commanded that the remaining brothers bring Binyamin as a gesture of good faith.

Knowing the power of the Egyptian, Yaakov wanted to appease the viceroy, who had taken his son Shimon as a hostage and had demanded that Binyamin be sent to him. So the great patriarch sent a variety of food gifts to this mysterious viceroy, who seemed to know everything about his family. Among the items that Yaakov sent was something that the Torah terms *botnim* (*Genesis 43:11*). Rashi says, "I don't know what *botnim* are," then adds that "Rabbi Meir explains them as pistachios, and I think they are persimmons."

When I was a child my rebbe told us, "You see? Rashi said, 'I don't know!'" We were supposed to learn something from that — although I was not sure exactly what until I heard the following story.

A group rabbinical students, gathered around a rabbi who had just emerged from a store in the Meah

Shearim section of Jerusalem. Craig, who was spending a year of Torah study in Israel after graduating from a co-ed Jewish high school, saw the scene out of the corner of his eye. Then he realized that a picture of the rabbi, who had attracted the attention of all the young scholars, hung on his classroom wall. Indeed, his favorite Rabbi could not stop singing the praises of this brilliant and equally humble Torah sage. In fact, even back in the States his own rabbi had talked about this great *tzaddik.* "Yes," Craig thought, "it is none other than Rabbi Shlomo Zalman Auerbach."

Realizing the opportunity, he quickly, raced over to participate in the conversation; he, too, wanted to speak to the great man.

The yeshiva students were peppering Rabbi Auerbach with complex Talmudic questions.

"How does one reconcile the opinion of *Rambam* with the *Gemora* in the third chapter of *Bava Kama*?" one asked.

"How can one answer the contradictory opinions of the *Shach* in *Choshen Mishpat*?" another demanded.

"Does the *Rav* concur with the ruling of the *Chazon Ish* regarding the completion of electrical circuits on the Sabbath and Festivals?" another probed.

To each young man the Sage had a simple reply.

"Look at the *Pischei Tshuva* in *Yoreh Deah,*" he nodded at one.

"The *Maharam Shif* asks your question in *Bava Kama,*" he smiled at the next, his complex Talmudic reasoning flowing effortlessly.

"Look in the 12th chapter of my work *Minchas Shlomo,*" he replied humbly. "I discuss it there in detail."

So it went: deep question; short answer. Eventually, some of the boys went away, and the crowd got smaller. Craig's mind raced. While he was no great student of the Talmud, and his knowledge of *Ivrit* was weak at best, he badly wanted to partake in the banter. But what could he ask this great scholar?

Suddenly, a warm hand was outstretched, and a broad smile appeared on Rabbi Auerbach's face.

Rabbi Auerbach was shaking his hand. A few of the older boys were watching the encounter of the *Gadol HaDor* (sage of the generation) and the American high-school graduate.

"And how can I help you?" asked the Rabbi.

Craig's mind raced. "Umm... umm," he stammered. He wanted so badly to ask an imposing Talmudic perplexity but he could not think of one. Suddenly, he came up with a less complex question.

"Is it true that Bazooka® Bubble Gum is really kosher in Israel?" he asked breathlessly.

Rav Shlomo Zalman stopped. He pondered. He shook his head. "This is something I really don't know," he said. "You have truly stumped me."

Craig went back to his yeshiva a different boy. He, a simple graduate of a Hebrew day school, had asked the generation's leading Sage a question that he could not answer! Thus encouraged, Craig got serious about Torah study. All his frustration about not understanding Talmudic complexities had dissipated. After all, the great Rabbi Auerbach could not answer his question!

When I learned this Rashi for the first time at the age of seven, I could not get over the fact that Rashi did not know something. I was even more amazed that although Rashi had two alternate explanations, he boldly opened his commentary by stating, "I don't know."

Rashi sends a message to every student. You can still be a Rashi — the single greatest commentator on the entire Torah, Prophets, and Talmud — and still not know the translation of a simple word! Rashi clearly says that one should not be afraid to declare on a tiny and perhaps insignificant translation — one that can be interpreted in a variety of ways, from pistachios to persimmons — "I don't know."

What is the exact reason for Rashi's declaration? Was he truly unable to translate the word? Or was he giving us the strength to continue even when we are stumped.

To tell you the truth, I really don't know.

Parshas Vayigash

For Crying Out Loud

It was a war of words, a battle of will, power, and courage. Who would blink first: Yehuda or Yosef?

This is the scenario. Before the brothers departed from Egypt, Yosef had surreptitiously planted his silver goblet in his brother Binyamin's sack. Not long after Yosef sent his brothers back to Canaan, his agents pursued them, arrested them, and accused them of robbery. Lo and behold, Binyamin was caught with the silver goblet. Brought back to the palace, Binyamin was sentenced by Yosef to eternal servitude. The other brothers were seemingly helpless.

Yehuda, having accepted full responsibility for Binyamin's safe return, pleaded with Yosef — while he also prepared to do battle. After all, he exclaimed, "How can I return to my father without my brother, lest I see the evil that will befall my father!" (*Genesis 44:34*)

When Yosef saw the depth of emotion that Yehuda and the brothers demonstrated for the youngest one, he could not continue his charade. Sending all the Egyptians from the room, he burst out, "I am Yosef! Is my father still alive?" (*Genesis 45:3*)

Hardly a commentary fails to expound upon the obvious question. Yosef was just told how eagerly Yaakov awaited the return of Binyamin. Therefore Yosef knew that Yaakov was alive. Why then did he ask the question?

It was to be an unparalleled Jewish wedding, as the daughter of Rabbi Chaim Elazar Schapiro, the

illustrious Munkacser Rebbe, was to marry the son of the Rebbe of Partzov. Both Chassidic dynasties were royal, aristocratic, and majestic. And the ceremony was to be equally regal. The bride and groom would ride in opulent carriages drawn by four white horses. The wedding meal was so large that every needy member of the community would be welcome to partake. It was the Jewish event of the century!

There was so much excitement that an actual news crew came to film the wedding, with the footage to be incorporated as part of pre-feature newsreels shown at American movie theatres across the Atlantic! "Imagine!" thought the reporters, "this will attract into theatres thousands of American Jews who had roots in Europe!" However, there was a difficulty: convincing the Munkacser Rebbe to speak for the cameras. The Rebbe, vehemently opposed to the frivolities and wanton ideas of the cinema, would not participate in a film. The producer assured the Rebbe, only his voice and not his face would be presented (an assurance that proved to be false, by the way).

"Rebbe," the producer cajoled, "this is a wonderful opportunity for you to talk to unimaginably large audiences about the Chassidic court of Munkacs! Think of how many Jews would be fascinated by your life's work. It would also be a wonderful opportunity to send your personal wishes to all your followers who have left Europe to go to America."

After much consideration, the Rebbe finally consented. The film, which still exists and is archived at the Museum of Jewish Heritage in New York City, caught the Rebbe speaking for the microphones — and for the camera that was obscured from his view. He was very brief. Tearfully, he repeated his message a few times and then stopped talking.

The American crew was excited. They were going to present the wedding with its entire mystique and majesty to American audiences.

However, when the wedding film was shown in American theatres the scene of the pomp and circumstance of the ceremony was a stark contrast to the

interview with the Rebbe. They did not see a jubilant Rabbi Schapiro toasting the large audience upon the joyous occasion. Instead, they saw Rabbi Schapiro pleading on the silver screen.

***"Yidden!"* he cried, *"Heet der Shabbos!"* (Jews! Keep the Sabbath!) Those were the only words that the Rebbe chose to speak. Then he turned his face and wept.**

Yosef had kept his emotions bottled up from the moment he saw his brothers enter Egypt until he revealed his identity in the privacy of his chambers. But throughout the entire ordeal there was one question he felt he had to ask. How is my father? Is he alive and well? Although the information was afforded him, he felt a responsibility to ask about his dear father's welfare. Therefore, the moment he was free to speak he instinctively asked, "Is my father still alive? How has he fared?" He did not chastise his brothers. He did not demand retribution. He did not seek vengeance. All he did was reveal his true feelings and ask the question that was on his heart and mind for 22 years. How is my father?

Parshas Vayechi

Calculated Doublespeak

There is an interesting Midrashic interpretation of two words in this portion that seems to contrast starkly with their simple meaning. In fact, on the surface the interpretation seems even to contradict the simple meaning!

Yaakov blessed Yosef's children, then told him, "As for me, I have given you [the city of] Shechem, one portion more than your brothers, which I took from the Emorite with my sword and with my bow" (*Genesis* 48:22).

Rashi explains that after Yosef's brothers attacked Shechem in response to the assault on their sister Dina, the Emorites, a neighboring country, tried to conquer Yaakov at his time of weakness, a military move similar to Jordan joining against Israel in the Six-Day War. The Emorites, like the Jordanians centuries later, were miraculously defeated.

Yaakov told Yoseph that he acquired those lands with his sword and bow. But Rashi and the *Targum Onkeles*, the latter known for his near-literal translation of the Torah, deviate from the literal, translating the words "bow and sword" differently. Rashi explains that they refer to wisdom and prayer, while the *Targum* explains the words as two forms of supplication.

Such allegorical interpretation is understandable. Prayer surely surpasses the pen in its might over the sword. And some prayers, like swords, are strong and sweeping and affect all those they strike. Other prayers, like arrows, travel a far distance to reach one specific point. The allegory is beautiful, but such translations naturally give rise to questions. To begin with, we know that Yaakov prayed. Of course, he prayed! Yaakov's prayers are documented throughout the Book of *Genesis*. He prayed during his encounters with all his adversaries. In this particular instance, however, he chose to talk to his son about his battle prowess. Why then would these two great commentators translate his discussions of the weapons of war as forms of prayer?

The Ponovezer Rav, Rabbi Yosef Kahaneman, of blessed memory, was renowned for his efforts to rebuild Torah out of the ashes of the Holocaust. Among his many achievements, he created the jewel in the crown of the Torah city B'nai Brak by building the Ponovez Yeshiva and its myriad affiliate institutions -- a yeshiva for pre-teens, another for young men, a third for married scholars. Rabbi Kahaneman also built the Batei Avos, a huge housing complex with hundreds of subsidized apartments for needy families. In addition, he built schools for orphaned boys and girls in B'nei Brak, Ashdod, and numerous other cities across the state of Israel.

Often, Rabbi Kahaneman visited wealthy patrons in the United States, Canada, South Africa, and Europe, appealing to them to contribute monies to the Ponovezer Institutions.

The story is told, perhaps apocryphally, that one particular donor once confronted Rabbi Kahaneman in jest.

"Why is it, Rabbi," the man wondered, "that all the other rabbis and *Roshei Yeshiva* who visit me never mention money? All they talk about is Torah and *mitzvos*. But you come here and cut right to the chase. You don't talk about Torah or *mitzvos.* Your appeal is direct and to the point. You come here and say that you need one hundred thousand dollars to finish a girls' school in Ashdod. That's fine. But why don't you also give me a speech about Torah, *mitzvos,* and Jewish continuity?"

Rabbi Kahaneman did not draw back. He took the man's hand and told him something very profound. "You know me well," he said. "Many fund raisers talk, 'Torah, Torah, Torah,' but they mean 'money, money, money.' I talk money, but I mean 'Torah, Torah, Torah.'"

Our *Chazal,* who understood the essence of Yaakov's being; who saw his deep faith while running from Esav, fighting with the angel, and confronting the tragedy of Shechem; and who appreciated his travail with Lavan; also understood quite well what his literal bow and sword were. Additionally, they were very comfortable with the greatness of Yaakov's persona, one steeped in a spirituality constantly connected to his Creator.

So they understood full well that when Yaakov said "sword" he meant the swift and sharp result of prayer, and when he said "bow and arrow" he meant the piercing cry of supplication.

All the words of our forebears, even the seemingly mundane words, are the foundation of our faith and filled with spiritual meaning. Everything they said and did pointed directly to the One Above.

Therefore, we must be suspect not of them, but of ourselves as temporal beings, when preaching prayer and espousing faith. Do we really mean prayer and faith — or are we just *talking* prayer and faith, but *thinking* bows and arrows?

ספר שמות

The Book of Exodus

Parshas Shemos

Growth Investment

It was a test for the ages. The mighty Pharaoh commanded the midwives *Shifra* and *Pooah,* known to us as Yocheved and her daughter Miriam, to kill all the boys born to Hebrew mothers. Not only did they ignore the edict, they countered it by nourishing the newborns with pacifying words and comforting amenities — food and drink. The *Midrash* tells us that they even cared for the sick and unhealthy babies as well, succoring them with prayers and nourishment. Hashem in heaven did not ignore their actions. Nevertheless, certain verses need some explanation. First, the Torah tells us, "And God rewarded the midwives, and the nation flourished and prospered." Only then does it add, "And it was as the midwives feared Hashem, and He made for them houses" *(Exodus 1:21-22).*

Rashi explains that both midwives were rewarded for their efforts with more than physical houses. They were well rewarded by Hashem with houses of *kohanim* and kings — with generations of priests and royalty. Those attributes are perpetuated only through the gender that the midwives actually saved — male Jewish children! A *kohen* can only be the son of a *kohen,* and a king can only be a male! Thus their actions merited an appropriate reward.

However, there seems to be an interruption in the order of the verses. The words "and the nation flourished" seem out of context. In fact, Rashi explains the verse as "And God rewarded the midwives" by asking, "What was the reward?" The response is, "He made for them houses." The words "and the nation flourished" possibly are part of the narrative, an historical footnote inserted into the middle of the episode of heroism and reward. Still, the simple, juxtaposed text needs clarification. Perhaps there is a way to explain the historical insert as part of the reward.

More than 12 years ago, my brother, Reb Zvi, and his wife had a beautiful little baby boy. He was truly beautiful. And he was truly little: five weeks premature and only two-and-a-half pounds.

For a while, it was touch and go. The prayers of a community and thousands of friends and relatives became the spiritual support systems that sustained the child's short breaths and his parents' deep hopes. For nearly two months, the baby endured in a neo-natal unit under the care of the most prestigious doctors and devoted nurses that the city of Chicago had to offer.

After the prayers, incubators, and devoted healthcare, the baby finally arrived home healthy. While the joy and gratitude to Hashem was overwhelming, the young father did not forget his appreciation to the mortal messengers, the entire medical and nursing staff who worked arduously, day and night, to help insure the newborn's health.

Reb Zvi wanted to express his appreciation in a very special way. He searched gift shops and bookstores for a proper memento to show his appreciation, but he could not come up with an appropriate gift.

A few days after the baby was brought home, the young father mentioned his dilemma to Rabbi Eliyahu Svei, *Rosh Yeshiva* of the Philadelphia Yeshiva.

"The nurses don't want perfume, and the doctors don't need pens," said Rabbi Svei. "What they want to see is the continued growth and health of your child. Every year, on his birthday, bring the child to the hospital and let the staff share in the joy of his success! That will be the most meaningful gift you can offer!"

Before the Torah mentions an additional reward bestowed upon the midwives, it alludes to the greater reward that they truly appreciated. Their efforts towards Jewish perpetuity were not in vain. The nation prospered. The young babies, whom they worked so diligently to sustain, grew up. They married, and they flourished. Because all the midwives wanted was the propagation of their nation — that was their first reward, and it was reward enough!

Yet there was more. The gift of Houses of Priesthood and Houses of Royalty were an added bonus incumbent upon God to deliver in the future — for the entire Jewish nation. But as far as the midwives were concerned, their reward was the joy in seeing that the children they delivered had flourished, and that the nation grew. All the risks they had endured were worth it for that knowledge alone.

Of course the Torah tells us that Hashem made good on His promises, the nation prospered, and the midwives enjoyed it. For them, that was the greatest reward. They did not need to exhilarate in a windfall profit: the priesthood and kingship were a bonus. Instead, they witnessed the fulfillment of their main objective. They saw real returns on a growth investment.

Parshas Va'eira

Hail to the Chief

Some people just never learn. For nearly a year, Pharaoh was literally plagued by every conceivable misfortune, yet he refused to let the Jewish people leave his land. Of course, he pleaded with Moshe during every plague to stop the great inconvenience, pain, and disaster that were befalling his country. He even promised to let the Jews go, yet he never admitted guilt — and never kept his word.

More than once, Pharaoh beseeched Moshe to end the plagues. "Pray for me and remove the frogs! I will let you serve your God in the desert" (*Exodus 8:4*). Sometimes, Pharaoh offered unrestricted freedom, only to renege when the plagues ceased. Never, except on one occasion, did he admit that God was correct and he was corrupt.

That exception was the plague of hail — a plague so powerful that even Hashem Himself categorized it in a unique way. Indeed, Moshe quoted Hashem to Pharaoh: "This time, I shall send all My plagues against your heart, upon your servants, and your people, so that you shall know that there is none like Me in the world" (*Exodus 9:14*). Why did Hashem consider the hail a more powerful act than turning water into blood, or bringing pestilence, wild animals, and frogs?

True, the hail did miraculously contain a fire ensconced in the ice, but all the plagues had miraculous attributes to them. Turning the great Nile River into blood is not an everyday occurrence, either! So what characteristics did the hail have to label it "all My plagues?"

Even more puzzling was Pharaoh's response. After the plague struck Egypt, he called Moshe and Ahron and told them,

"This time I have sinned, Hashem is righteous, and I and my people are the wicked ones" (*Exodus 9:27*). What caused Pharaoh to utter those submissive words at that particular time? Hadn't he already seen blood, frogs, pestilence, boils, wild animals, and a host of other miraculous misfortunes befall his people? What was so special about the fire and ice that fell from the heavens that seared even that man's cruel temper?

William and his Aunt Caroline were constantly feuding. Actually, William was jealous of his aunt's popularity and social status in the New York of the late 1890s. Compared to her, he was considered a social outcast, and was never invited to any of her lavish parties. That would have been bad enough, but having to live next door to her was too much for William to bear. The sight of elegant carriages arriving and departing made him seethe.

Yet he could do nothing. At least he did nothing until the family fortune was distributed and he received 100 million dollars. Then he knew what to do. He decided to rip down his mansion and build the biggest guest house in New York. It would have 530 rooms, 350 baths, and an astounding 970 employees. It would simply be the grandest, most elegant building of its kind in the world. More carriages would pull up to his hotel in a day than to his aunt's mansion in a month! Her home would pale in comparison, and the tumult of it all would force her to move.

William was right. Chagrined, Aunt Caroline moved way north of her nephew's house. And then she ripped down her old home, too. With the mere 50 million that she received, she too, decided to build a hotel on the site of her old mansion! It would be even more elegant, with nicer rooms and better service than her nephew's. She would have done it, too, creating two adjacent, competing hotels, if not for the wisdom of William's own hotel manager. He got the two feuding relatives together and explained that hostility is not the way to success.

"If you two could just work together and adjoin the two hotels as one, it would become the most outstanding and influential accommodation on earth," he explained.

They listened and followed his instructions, including his advice that they make certain every opening between the structures could be sealed in case of a renewed falling out. But in the end, William Waldorf and his aunt, Caroline Astor, decided to bury the hatchet and replace it with a hyphen. And so they created the world's most luxurious accommodation — The Waldorf-Astoria Hotel.

There are many opposing forces in the world. However, when they work in tandem they can be the most powerful force imaginable. During this plague, fire and ice, two opposing forces in the world of nature, disregarded their differences in the service of the Supreme Commander. When Hashem announced that He would send all of His plagues, he was referring to conflicting forces that would work harmoniously. After that, even Pharaoh was sensible enough, albeit for a short moment, to see his frailty and delusions.

When even the worst of men see fire and ice work together on one mission, there is nothing he can do but watch in amazement and admit, "Hashem is the righteous one, and I and my people are the wicked ones." When opposing opinions and diverse forces unite for one objective — to do the will of Hashem — they are as unstoppable as the hail that brought Pharaoh to his knees. And their unity inspired even the brashest of skeptics to say, "Hashem is the *tzadik,* and it is I and my nation who are the sinners."

Parshas Bo

Oy Vey!

"Don't get mad," said the philosophers of the '80s, "get even." Of course, the Almighty's objective of the Ten Plagues was not to get even *per sé* with the nation that had enslaved His people. The plagues were meant to teach a moral lesson. *Midah k'neged midah.* Measure for measure. Indeed, the *Tana D'bei Eliyahu,* Chapter Seven, correlates the results of the Ten Plagues as direct punishment for Egyptian crimes against the Jewish people.

In fact, the concept of *midah k'neged midah* was present in all the plagues, each corresponding to a different form of subjugation endured by the Jews. For example, the most famous — the Egyptians drowning in the *Yam Suf* — was Hashem's direct response to the Egyptians throwing Jewish babies into the Nile

So perhaps we could say that in a slight way the Jewish people got even. There is, however, no scriptural evidence that they got mad. In fact, each time Moshe went to Pharaoh, the negotiations were calm — nearly serene!

"'Let My people serve Me,'" Moshe commanded in God's name. When Pharaoh refused, his obstinacy was met with a clear and calculated threat. "If you refuse to let the people leave," Moshe said, "I will send the following plague in your land."

And so it went. Sometimes a plague immediately followed a warning, other times plagues came with no warning at all. Then, when Pharaoh found Moshe and arranged for a cessation of each scourge, Pharaoh reneged on his commitment soon after.

Moshe became frustrated; perhaps he even became impatient. But he displayed no anger until the final plague. Then he not only got even, he got mad.

Moshe warned Pharaoh with the words of Hashem, "At about midnight, I will go out in the midst of Egypt, and every firstborn in the land of Egypt shall die" (*Exodus 11:4-5*). Though Moshe then detailed the ramifications of the plague, he was answered by Pharaoh's apathetic response. Finally, the Torah tells us, "Moshe left Pharaoh in burning anger" (*Exodus 11:8*).

This, of course, raises a question. Why only then did Moshe storm out in a rage? Was he not accustomed to the callous recklessness of the Egyptian leader? What distressed him during this last encounter more than in any of the previous ones?

The great physicist Albert Einstein escaped the Nazi inferno to find a haven in the United States. During World War II, his letter to President Roosevelt initiated the effort that spurred the creation of the atomic bomb. Einstein knew the destructive power that his ideas could potentially release, and indeed his theory of relativity was a prime factor in the bomb's development. Nevertheless, when Einstein heard in an August 6, 1945, radio broadcast that an atomic device was dropped on the city of Hiroshima, he reacted with stunned silence. After a moment of somber reflection he only found two words to say, "*Oy vey!*"

Rabbi Shimon Schwab, of blessed memory, explains that Moshe had patience with Pharaoh up to a point. Moshe knew that throughout the ordeal the reckless king's obstinate decisions caused a great amount of discomfort to his people. Indeed, even when his advisors pleaded, "How long will this man [Moshe] be an obstacle, let them [the Jews] serve their God," Pharaoh refused. And his recalcitrance brought plagues of pestilence, boils, locust, and darkness — in addition to blood, frogs, and lice. All of these afflictions were vastly uncomfortable — but not fatal. Even the fiery hail did not harm those God-fearing Egyptians who sought shelter.

Yet the last plague, the killing of the firstborn, had the most devastating ramifications. It meant the deaths of thousands of Egyptians, "from the firstborn son of Pharaoh to that of the maidservant who was behind the millstone." The plague's destruction was so powerful that the Torah says "such has never been and will never be again" (*Exodus 11:6*).

For his part, Pharaoh could have stopped the imminent tragedy with one simple word — "go." Yet he chose to remain steadfast in his denial, bringing the downfall of his people and the death of thousands of firstborn children. And that callous and reckless behavior infuriated Moshe, whose compassion for the simplest beings earned him the right to be the leader of the Jewish nation. As such, the stark contrast displayed by his nemesis appalled him to the point of rage.

The Torah commands us, "do not to hate the Egyptian, for you were a sojourner in his land" (*Deuteronomy 23:8*). As we see, the Torah's attitude toward the nation that held us captive is even more compassionate than that of its own leaders.

It has not stopped despite the passage of 3,300 years. Barbaric leaders — clearly reminiscent of the Pharaoh who destroyed his own family to save his ego — continue to egg on simple people throughout the world, forcing them to act in terribly self-destructive ways. That's enough to make anybody — even the most humble man who ever lived — very upset.

PARSHAS B'SHALACH

Input...Output

The sea had split. The enemy had drowned. The Jews were free. And then the problems began.

The newly liberated nation was stranded in a scorching desert facing an unending landscape of uncertainty. Taskmasters no longer responded to their cries — Hashem did, with protection and shelter on every level. But the Jews were still not satisfied. They were hungry. "If only we had died in the land of Egypt. Why did you liberate us to die in the desert?" they cried to Moshe (*Exodus 16:3*).

Hashem answered with a most miraculous and equally mysterious celestial gift. Manna fell from the heavens. The people accepted it with piqued curiosity, and while the dew-covered matter satiated their hunger, they were not sure exactly what they were eating. "Each man said to his friend, *'mahn hu!'* For they did not know what it was" (*Exodus 16:15*). From then on the Torah refers to the celestial delicacy as *mahn.* Indeed, the commentaries explain that the word *manna* is a Hebrew-Egyptian form of the word "what."

At first, the Torah only discusses the physical attributes of the manna: "it was like a thin frost on the earth" (v. 14). Later, the Torah tells us that on Shabbos the manna did not fall. A double portion fell on Friday, with the extra portion allotted for Shabbos. In referring specifically to the manna of Shabbos, the Torah tells us that "the Children of Israel named it manna, and it tasted like a cake fried in honey" (v. 31). Later, however, the Torah describes the manna's taste differently: "it tasted like dough kneaded with oil" (*Numbers 11:8*).

Questions abound. Why the quick transformation of the Jews' attitude toward the manna? Before Shabbos people asked, "what is it?" On Shabbos they did not ask, "what is it?" Rather, they declared what it was and named the heavenly delicacy "it is 'what (manna).'"

So why did the Jews wait until Shabbos to describe concretely this miraculous edible with the title manna — the 'what' food?

And why does the Torah wait to describe the manna's taste until Shabbos? And when did it taste sweet and when only like oily dough?

In his book, *Once Upon A Shtetl,* Rabbi Chaim Shapiro tells of the town of Lomza, where there was a group of woodcutters hired by the townsfolk to cut down trees for firewood. The strong laborers swung their axes and hit the trees, all while shouting a great cry "Hah!" with each blow. In every case, the timing had to be flawless. If the shouted "Hah!" came a split-second early, or a split-second after the blades hit the trees, it would be but a worthless shout that would not aid the lumberjacks at all.

Each year, Zelig the *meshugener,* a once-successful businessman who had lost his mind with the loss of a young daughter, accompanied the woodcutters on their quest. He stood in the background, and, precisely as the axes hit the trees, he, too, shouted at the top of his lungs "Hah!"

When it was time to get paid, the deranged Zelig also stood in line. "I deserve some silver coins!" he exclaimed. "After all, without my shouting, the wood chopping would not be as effective!"

The case was brought before the Chief Rabbi of Lomza, who looked at the five lumberjacks and then at the *meshugener.*

"Listen carefully, Zelig," the Rabbi said. He then took 10 silver pieces in his hand and jingled them loudly. They made a loud clanging noise. Then he gave each woodsman two silver pieces. He turned to Zelig and smiled. "The men who invested the labor get the coins, and, you, Zelig, who invested the sound, get the sound of the coins!"

Hashem, in His infinite wisdom, began our lessons in living through our daily fare. The Talmud states that the taste of the manna was integrally linked to the taster's thoughts. If one thought of steak, the manna tasted like steak; if one thought of borscht, the manna tasted like borscht. The Talmud also adds that to small children the manna tasted like dough, but to scholars it tasted like honey. The Malbim explains that to scholars, whose thoughts are sweet as honey, the manna tasted like honey. For when one thought of honey, he tasted honey. And when one thought blandly, however, he had a bland taste.

Indeed, the Chofetz Chaim was once asked, "what happened if one thought of nothing?" He answered very profoundly: "If one thought of nothing, then one tasted nothing!"

During the week, the Jews had the manna but did not realize its great potential — which is why, the Malbim explains, it tasted only like oily dough. But on *Shabbos,* a day filled with wondrous relaxation, the minds of the nation were filled with heavenly thoughts — which, in turn, were reflected in the sweet taste of honey-flavored manna.

So perhaps on *Shabbos* the Jewish people realized the important lesson of life. The questions we face should not be addressed as eternally mysterious; we cannot face the unknown with the question, "what is it?" Rather, we can define our destiny and challenge our uncertainties. We can say, "It is what!"

The lesson goes further: you take out of life exactly what you put in! Life presents us many opportunities. We can approach those moments with lofty thoughts, and see, smell, and taste its sweetness. Or we can see nothing, think nothing, and taste nothing. We can chop hard and reap the benefits of our labor, or we can *kvetch* and only enjoy the echoes of our emptiness.

Parshas Yisro

Return to Sender

Yisro is the portion in which the people of Israel arrived at their spiritual, intellectual, and moral destination. It is the portion in which former Hebrew slaves chose to become the Chosen People, having accepted the responsibilities — and accountabilities — of God's 613 *mitzvos.* In *Yisro,* the Jews accepted the Torah at Mount Sinai.

It did not come easy. Hashem prefaced His Torah with an overpowering charge. He sent Moshe to speak to both the men and the women. "You shall be to Me a kingdom of ministers and a holy nation" (*Exodus 19:6*).

Accepting the Torah included the responsibilities of a holy nation — a new moral divining rod in a world fraught with immorality. But the Jews were up to the challenge, and they responded as such.

They did not murmur their response, nor did they mumble their acceptance. The Jews affirmed their agreement in unison — with words that resound throughout history as the battle cry of Jewish faith. They shouted in unison, "All that Hashem has commanded, we shall do!" (*Exodus 19:8*) The response, declaring total submission to Torah dictates, was proudly noted by the Almighty, Who handed the Jews a most-chosen-nation status through all their ordeals.

But Moshe did not look up to heaven with a contented smile, as if he were a proud brother sharing *nachas* with a Father watching from the bleachers. The Torah tells us, "and Moshe related the words of the people to Hashem" (*Exodus19:9*). Moshe returned to the Master of the Universe and reported the good news: he repeated their response, verbatim, to Hashem.

The question is obvious. Moshe knew, perhaps better than any mortal being, that every action, gesture, and thought of every inhabitant of this planet is duly recorded by the Almighty. Why, then, did he report back their response? Hashem was well aware of the enthusiasm and willing acceptance of the people. Furthermore, by telling us that Moshe went back to Hashem, isn't the Torah opening a Pandora's Box? Could one possibly infer that Hashem needed Moshe to find out the response? Obviously, there is a deeper lesson to be learned.

When a baby is born in New York State, tests are administered to determine if the child has any genetic diseases. Among the procedures are tests for histadinemia, a condition which causes excessive levels of the protein histadine to build up in the blood, thereby damaging the nervous system and causing retardation. Given the condition's severity, it must be addressed immediately.

Ten days after a baby was born to a young couple, the hospital frantically tracked down the parents to tell them that their child had a histadine level of 12 — and to bring him back immediately! (A histadine level of 1 or 2 points is considered normal.) The father instantly called his *Rebbe,* Rabbi Yaakov Kamenetzky, of blessed memory, who had been the *sandek* at the baby's *bris* just two days before.

Reb Yaakov said he would pray for the child, who had appeared fine. Then he told the young man to insist that the histadine test be repeated before any treatment was administered.

The parents rushed back to Bellevue Hospital, where they were greeted by an assortment of doctors, nurses, nutritionists, and therapists. The staff wanted to admit the newborn into the hospital immediately. They warned that if the baby was not admitted, permanent brain damage could result.

The parents insisted that the test be re-administered, to which the doctors grudgingly replied, "We will re-do the test, but understand that these tests are extremely accurate. We never get a false reading."

They re-administered the procedure and came out with a totally different figure. The histadine level was a bit over one! After further review, they realized that the first test was not off — the technician was! He put the decimal in the wrong place. The original reading should not have been 12, but rather 1.2!

The couple, quite upset about the unnecessary scare and trauma, drove with the baby straight to the home of Rabbi Kamenetzky to inform him that the whole ordeal was a mistake. Reb Yaakov, who was elated at the news, held the young father and kissed him. "Thank you for coming and telling me the good news," the Torah sage said. "So many people just tell me their *tzorus,* they ask me for advice, even for prayers, but when things get better, I never find out. I am left bearing the burden of their worries."

Moshe knew that Hashem heard the answer of the Jewish nation more loudly than he did. But Moshe was sent on a mission, and he had the responsibility to convey the good news. In addition, he wanted to send the Jewish people a message as well. He taught his people that before a person can receive the Torah, he must be a good messenger. Because everything that we study — everything we do on this earth — is but a message that must be accounted to Hashem. Indeed, even if Hashem knows what we are doing, we must return with a report of accomplishment. So Moshe taught us that *derech eretz* must not only precede learning Torah, it precedes giving it as well.

Parshas Mishpatim

Romancing the Enemy

Receiving the Ten Commandments may have been the pinnacle of the Jewish experience, but by no means did Judaism end there. In this portion, the Torah details myriad pecuniary laws, including torts and damage laws, as well as the laws of physical injury and impairment compensation. Surely a nation that had just emerged from brutal enslavement needed a strict code to discipline its freedom. But what is puzzling is the order of the laws. The first commandments, a set of more than 50 intricate laws detailing virtually every aspect of life's complexities, concern servitude. *Parshas Mishpatim* begins with the words, "When you will acquire a Jewish servant, he shall serve six years, and on the seventh he shall go free" (*Exodus 21:2*).

It is astounding! The Jews had just spent the last 210 years in a foreign land, the greater part of those years as slaves. Why would they have even entertained thoughts of taking servants? Shouldn't the first laws have dictated compassion for other humans, thus enforcing the total equality of an entire, newly liberated nation? Furthermore, of all the ideas discussed with these former slaves, wouldn't the very concept of masters and servants have been loath to them? Why, then, are those laws given first?

When Shalom, who had never left his small hamlet in Yemen, was finally able to leave his home for Israel, back in the early '50s, the airplane ride, Shalom's first experience with any technology, was absolutely frightening. Not only was it the first time

he had ever seen an airplane, it was the first time he had even seen steps! Upon his arrival at Lod airport, the mad rush of taxis truly terrified him, but his cousin Moshe, who lived on a small settlement not far from the Lod train station, eased his fears by sending a driver to pick Shalom up from the airport.

The driver dropped off the dazed immigrant near the station and gave him directions to the farm. "Walk beside the train tracks for about a mile. You can't miss it," he exclaimed.

Shalom, who had never seen train tracks in his life, and had never even seen a train, chose to walk right between the two iron tracks. After about five minutes, he saw a giant machine bearing down directly upon him.

"Toot toot!" the train whistled. The conductor waved frantically at Shalom as he tried to stop the mammoth machine. Shalom froze as he stood aghast at this marvelous site. "Toot toot!" the whistle went once more. The train could not stop! At the last moment, Shalom quickly jumped out of the way, and the train hurtled by, missing him by a hair. So fast was the enormous machine traveling, that Shalom was knocked down by the rush of air accompanying the speeding train. As he picked himself up, all he could see was the enormous black beast fleeing down the track, mocking him with a shrill, "toot toot."

Bruised and shaken, he hobbled the rest of the way along the tracks until he arrived at his cousin's farm.

Moshe saw his cousin, Shalom, and could not begin to imagine what happened to him. But Moshe figured there was time to talk over a glass of hot tea. He put a shiny black kettle to boil on the stove, but no sooner had the kettle begun to whistle when poor Shalom jumped from his chair and began to shout. He grabbed a broom that stood in the corner of the kitchen and swung wildly at the whistling teapot, smashing it with all his might.

"Believe me," he yelled in terror, "I know! You have to destroy these monsters while they are still young!"

The Torah understood the Jewish nation's feelings toward its slave experience. Slavery is loathsome and reprehensible. The impact of that experience could have created an unhealthy attitude toward servitude — even in a humane and benevolent environment. Therefore, the Torah immediately detailed its very humanitarian laws of servitude — clearly and openly. There can be six years of service and no more. A servant can never be humiliated or degraded. In fact, the rules of Jewish servitude are so humane that the Talmud surmises that "whoever owns a servant has actually acquired a master. If there is only one pillow in the home — the master must to give it to his servant!"

Therefore, instead of shirking from the difficult task of specifying the laws of servitude or pushing them to a back burner, the Torah discusses those laws first — without any apologies.

In an imperfect world there are imperfect situations. People steal. They owe money. They must work for others to pay off debt or pay back money they have swindled. Nevertheless, when the problems and injustices of life are dealt with in a Torah way, the imperfect world can come a little closer to perfection.

Parshas Terumah

Support System

The *Aron Kodesh* in the *Mishkan* contained the most precious spiritual gift that was ever transmitted by Omnipotent to mortal — the two *Luchos*, the tablets Hashem handed to Moshe at Sinai. Therefore, given the extraordinary nature of the object, its receptacle had to be worthy of housing it. The *Aron* had to be intricately constructed, with its symbolism as meticulously configured as its beautiful design. In fact, the *Aron* consisted of three contiguous boxes of gold, wood, and gold, each inserted in the other. It also featured a golden crown bordering its edge, and a golden cover adorned with cherubim. These angelic figures faced each other with wings spread, representing the profound mutual love of a nation and its Creator.

But a seemingly insignificant item connected with the *Aron* has perhaps the greatest symbolism of all the many peripheral adornments. The Torah tells us that the *Aron* was to be fitted with gold-plated wooden staves. Then Moshe is told, "You shall insert the staves in the rings on the Ark, with which to carry the ark" (*Exodus 25:14*). The Torah goes on to state: "The staves shall remain in the rings of the Ark; they shall not be removed" (*Exodus 25:15*).

Our Sages explain that the Torah is thus stating a prohibition against anyone removing the staves that were used to carry the Ark from place to place during the Jews' sojourn in the desert and beyond. What needs examination, however, is the phraseology of the command. When referring to the staves, instead of commanding, "You shall not remove them," the Torah declares, "they shall not be removed." Why didn't the Torah just command, "the staves shall remain in the Ark; you shall not remove them"? By stating, "they shall not be removed" it seems that instead of talking to the Jewish nation, the Torah is talking to history.

Can it be that the Torah is foreshadowing the relationship between the Holy Ark itself and the staves that carry it? What important symbolism do the staves bear that intrinsically connects them with the Holy Ark they are meant to support? Can seemingly insignificant staves actually become part and parcel of the Ark's very essence?

During World War II, many young Jewish children were harbored by various monasteries throughout Europe. At the end of the war, the Vaad Hatzalah sent representatives to the monasteries to try and reclaim the orphaned children and bring them back to their heritage. With some children, the task was easy. But for others, it was not, for many of the children who found refuge did so at a young age — and they had but few recollections of their birthright.

When Rabbi Eliezer Silver, from Cincinnati, Ohio, and a very influential member of the Vaad, came to a particular hermitage in the Alsace-Lorraine region of France, he was met with hostility. "You can be sure, Rabbi, if we had Jews here, we would surely hand them back to you immediately!" the monk in charge exclaimed. "However, unfortunately for you, we have no Jewish children here."

The monk then gave Rabbi Silver a list of refugees and told him that they were all Germans. "The Schwartzs are German Schwartzs," the monk said. "The Schindlers are German Schindlers. And the Schwimmers are German Schwimmers."

Yet Rabbi Silver had been told that there were close to 10 Jewish children in that hermitage, and so he was not convinced. He then asked the monk if he could say a few words to the children as they went to sleep. Cautiously, the monk agreed.

Later that evening, Rabbi Silver returned with two aides. Just before the children were about to go to sleep, they were brought into a large room. Rabbi

Silver entered, and in the sing-song that is so familiar to hundreds of thousands of Jewish children across the globe, he began to chant, *"Shema Yisrael Ado..."*

Unexpectedly — in mid sentence — he stopped. Suddenly, from six children in the room, the continuation of that most powerful verse rang out in harmonious unison, *"...noi Elokainu!"* And together with Rabbi Silver the six boys all sang the very words that their parents sang to their deaths: *"Hashem Echad!"*

Rabbi Silver looked at the exuberance in the young children's eyes. He saw the tears streaming down their faces. And then he turned to the priest, whose shock could not mask his clear discomfort.

"These are our children," the Rabbi said softly. "I appreciate your harboring them during the war. But now it is time for them to come home."

The children were redeemed, placed in Jewish homes, and raised as Jewish children of whom their martyred parents would be proud.

When the Torah talks about the peripherals that help bear the burden of the *Aron,* in a unique way perhaps it is making a powerful prophecy in addition to a strong regulation. "In the rings of the ark the staves shall remain — they shall never leave!" Possibly that is more than a command. It is a prediction!

The wooden staves adapted to carry the message of Torah — the tunes, the customs, and the small nuances — are much more than gold-plated sticks. They may not be as holy as the Ark itself, but they will never leave its sides. They will be remembered long after the *Aron* has been captured. They will be cherished long after the golden Ark has been buried. And it may very well be that when the cherished handles of those staves, jutting ever so slightly from the ground, are pulled out from the mire, the entire Torah will eventually be raised with them.

Parshas Tezaveh

The Heart Before the Force

It is not easy to build a Sanctuary in the desert. And it may even be more difficult to adorn the *Kohanim* who serve in beautiful vestments that both symbolize deep spirituality while depicting splendor and glory. Indeed, it takes more than golden threads and fine tapestry. It takes more than the ability to weave and design ornate garments. Instead, it requires devotion, and it takes heart. Not ordinary heart. Not the heart that pennant winners have, or that athletic coaches call for. It takes a special type of heart, one that is filled with wisdom — Divine wisdom. That is why Hashem commanded Moshe to gather "all the wise-hearted people whom I have invested with a spirit of wisdom" to make the priestly garments (*Exodus 28:3*).

Yet the Torah seems unclear. Were these select people Divinely ordained with a spirit of wisdom for this particular mission, or were those intrinsically "wise-hearted" people imbued with an extra "spirit of wisdom"?

If the former is correct, then what did Hashem add, and when did He invest His spirit of wisdom in them? And if all their wisdom was Divinely gifted, why then didn't Hashem simply ask Moshe to "gather all the people in whom I have invested a spirit of wisdom?"

Rav Sholom Shwadron, of blessed memory, the *Maggid* of Jerusalem, once told a story about the famed Dubno Maggid, Rabbi Yaakov Kranz.

The Dubno Maggid once spoke in a town, and a few *maskilim* (members of the enlightenment movement) attended. After the talk, one of the cynics, who

was completely unaffected by the *Maggid's* warm and inspiring message, approached the famed *Maggid.* "The Sages tell us," the skeptic began, "that 'words from the heart, penetrate the heart.' Rabbi," he snickered, "I assume that you spoke from your heart. Your words, however, have had no impact on me whatsoever! How can that be? Why didn't your words penetrate my heart?"

Rabbi Kranz smiled. In his usual fashion, he began with a parable. "A simpleton once went by the workplace of a blacksmith, who was holding a large bellows. After a few squeezes, the flames of the smith's fire danced with a rage. The simple man, who always found it difficult to start a fire in his own fireplace, marveled at the contraption. He immediately purchased the amazing invention. Entering his home, he smugly announced, "I just discovered how to make a raging fire with the simple squeeze of a lever!"

He set a few logs in the cold fireplace and began to push the two ends of the bellows together. Nothing happened. The logs lay cold and lifeless. Embarrassed, the man returned to the blacksmith and explained his predicament. "I want a refund!" he shouted. "This blower doesn't work!"

"You yokel," the experienced blacksmith laughed. "You were blowing on cold logs! You must start a small fire on your own! If you don't start with a spark, the fire will never erupt!"

The *Maggid* turned toward the *maskil* and shook his head sadly. "If there is no spark, the largest bellows will not make a fire."

In telling Moshe whom to choose for the sacred task of designing the *Mishkan,* the Torah tells us how, and in whom, God invests. He wanted people who were imbued with a *ruach chachmah* — a spirit of wisdom. But he prefaced the statement by telling us how one receives spiritual wisdom. Indeed, the gift of spiritual wisdom is not bestowed on just anyone. Hashem looks for those who have wisdom of heart — those who understand what it means to be kind, compassionate, and loyal. Indeed, those who have the devotion to His will, and the desire for more enlightenment, will receive His ordination. Clearly, the people who were imbued with Hashem's Divine spirit previously had a spark. And from that spark grew a force — a Divine force — that propelled wise hearts into a Divine spirit of wisdom.

Hashem tells us that we must begin the process on our own. If we supply the heart, He will supply the power — so that we can have deep spiritual, even holy insight. He will supply the force. We must make sure, however, that we put the heart before the force.

Parshas Ki Sisa

Higher than Sinai

In the aftermath of the sin of the Golden Calf, Moshe's mortality was transformed to immortality in this portion as (anthropomorphic as it may sound) he got God to change His mind. Hashem, who had threatened to destroy the Jewish People after the Golden Calf, finally assured Moshe that His presence will accompany them on their sojourn.

But Moshe, it seemed, was still not satisfied. In what appeared as a daring move, he asked Hashem for more. Not only did Moshe want assurances of the Divine Presence's accompaniment, he asked Hashem to "show me Your glory" (*Exodus 33:18*). For Moshe, it was not enough that Hashem forgave the Jews for the most audacious sin of their young history. It was not enough that He assured them that He would guide them in the desert. Moshe wanted more! He wanted to connect the corporeal with the Omnipotent in a way never done before. He wanted to feast his soul on the most spiritual meal ingested through human vision. He wanted to see God. To that, Hashem explained that it is impossible to see Him and live. The human soul cannot be confined to a spatial-temporal existence after it has experienced the endless world of infinite spirituality. And thus the answer was, "No. You may, however, see My back" *(Exodus 33:20-23*).

Of course, the concept of God's "face," as opposed to His "back," fills tomes of commentators, from those who analyze textual references to the great Kabbalists, and it certainly cannot be digested here! What we can understand, however, is Moshe's persistence. Why was he dissatisfied with God's initial acquiescence? What propelled him, after almost losing the Jewish People, to ask to see the great bond of God to His creations?

Lou Maidenbaum, former executive of Met Foods, brought the Gedaliah Maidenbaum Preparatory School Division of Yeshiva of South Shore into existence. Before passing away, he was confined to a hospital in Miami Beach.

Even in his sick bed he never lost his spunk, charm, or desire to live life to its fullest. A week before he passed away, Lou was in his hospital room and experienced some discomfort. He pressed the button for a nurse, but no one came. Five minutes later, he rang again. Still no response. He tried two more times and then decided a new tactic.

He picked up the telephone and dialed 3 digits: 9-1-1.

"Emergency services," a woman said. "What is the problem?"

"I'm having difficulty breathing" Lou gasped.

"Where are you calling from?" she asked.

"Mount Sinai Hospital, Room 321," he said.

"Mount Sinai Hospital?" the incredulous dispatcher repeated. "What are you calling us for? You're in the hospital already!"

Lady," he shouted to the operator, "this is my life we're talking about. And if this is the way I'll get the best response, then I'm calling 911!"

Moshe knew that he had been on Sinai with God, receiving the Torah. However, that was not enough. Moshe was not complacent about his accomplishment; nor was he content with being the transmitter of eternity. He wanted more! He wanted to attain the highest possible level of mortal achievement. He wanted to see God. Moshe wanted to feast spiritually on the face of the Omnipotent. As such, Moshe was only concerned to attain the greatest degree of spirituality that he possibly could reach. There was nothing else on his mind or in his soul. To that, Hashem responded that if such a level would be attained, Moshe's soul would flee from its mortal constraints and refuse to re-enter a corporeal being. "No man shall see Me and live"

(*Exodus 33:20*). So Moshe had to concede, accepting the highest level the physical body could endure.

In Moshe's quest to go higher than Sinai he taught us a great lesson. No matter what level you think you are on, if you are standing on earth, you must reach for the mountain; and when you are standing on the mountain, you must reach for the clouds. And if you are standing on a cloud, you must reach for the stars.

Parshas Vayakhel

More? Then Enough!

In a magnanimous show of unity, men and women of all tribes of the Jewish People brought together their hearts, minds, and pockets to complete the *Mishkan.* In this and the next portion, the Torah summarizes the accomplishments of the nation by detailing the work that was done by Betzalel and his host of artisans and craftsmen who were filled with the Heavenly spirit.

Moshe declared the success of the campaign and the generosity of the donors by announcing, "the work (and contributions) had been enough for all the work, to do it — and there was extra" (*Exodus 36:7*).

The detail is telling: not only was there enough for the completion of the task — there was extra.

Many commentaries are concerned about Moshe's seemingly strange expression. "There was enough, and there was extra." After all, if there was enough, then there was not extra. And if there was extra, then it should not have been called enough! The Torah could just as well have stated, "There were extra contributions of work and material for the work that was needed."

It seems that only by having more than enough, only by having extra gifts, that there was actually enough. Is that possible?

President John F. Kennedy loved to tell the story of a political battle for the mayoralty of the small manufacturing city of Fall River, Massachusetts.

The candidates scoured the industrial community for support, each pledging prosperity, growth, and increased productivity. But general promises would

not persuade the voters. The candidates then talked to people as if each vote would truly decide the election. In turns out that they were right.

The Fall River mayoralty was the tightest election in Massachusetts history. During the vote counting, the candidates sat nervously with their supporters awaiting the final tally. It took days to declare, and weeks finally to confirm, that the winner of the mayoral race was actually decided by one vote!

But the winner's jubilation was muted only days after the results were declared — because everyone in the town reminded him, "It was my vote that got you elected!"

The *Sichos Tzadikim* explains that Moshe felt the pride involved in building the *Mishkan;* yet despite the enormity of the accomplishment, his feelings were tempered by his great personal humility. Had there been exactly enough gold, silver, copper, and other materials contributed in order to complete the construction, then perhaps a false sense of pride may have crept in — for Moshe as well other Jews.

"If it were not for me," some may have thought, "there would be no *Mishkan!* I gave the contribution that turned the tide!" Everyone would have pinned the success on his or her copper or silver or gold.

So the only way this false pride could have been avoided was if there were a bit more given to the cause than actually was needed. Only then would the Jewish nation not merely have had a *Mishkan,* but they would also have had an edifice bereft of individual haughtiness. Therefore, only when there was a bit more given than actually needed, did Moshe feel that he truly had enough!

When we face extreme situations, and we contribute to their positive resolutions, it is important to realize that we are merely messengers. If Hashem wants success, it will come without us as well.

In that vein, each contribution will be even more pure, for it will have every good attribute and will be missing only one ingredient — a false sense of conceit. Only then, it will not just be enough, it will be more.

Parshas Pekudei

Letting Go

The *Mishkan* is completed, and the Torah recaps the stunning accomplishment. "These are the reckonings of the *Mishkan,* the Tabernacle of Testimony that was reckoned through Moshe's bidding. And Betzalel, son of Uri, son of Chur, did everything that Hashem commanded Moshe" (*Exodus 38:21-22*).

The Torah calls the *Mishkan* a Tabernacle of Testimony. To what is it testifying? Architectural ability? A fund-raising phenomenon? Or perhaps something even loftier?

Rashi tells us that the *Mishkan,* in fact, testified that Hashem forgave the Jewish people for the sin of the Golden Calf.

Yet that statement raises questions. Forgiveness only occurs when it is accompanied by the correction of a misdeed. Indeed, each iniquity needs direct redress. Stinginess is forgiven with acts of munificence. Sins of uncontrolled rage are forgiven only when the transgressor acts with undeviating gentleness. And so on.

What connection does the building of the *Mishkan* have with creating the Golden Calf? And why is the completion of the *Mishkan* a testimony to absolution?

The second verse is also confusing. "Betzalel did what Hashem told Moshe." Did Betzalel not do what Moshe told him? It seems that the artisan jumped the chain of command. It should have stated that "Betzalel did what Moshe told him."

Dr. Abraham Twerski, in his book *Do Unto Others,* relates an amazing story that he personally experienced.

Early in his career, Dr. Twerski taught students by having them accompany him through psychiatric

institutions. There, he introduced the young observers to live subjects rarely seen outside textbooks.

In one chronic-care facility, Dr. Twerski pointed out a most difficult case — a male patient whom no doctor was able to cure. The man was mute and would not communicate. He had entered the facility 52 years earlier and was suffering from strange schizophrenic-like symptoms. Immediately following breakfast, he would go into the corner of the large community room, contort his arms, palms outstretched in an upward manner, and stand there until lunch. After lunch, he would resume his position until bedtime. No treatment — not medication, shock therapy, or psychotherapy — was able to get the man off his feet. Indeed, his condition was so severe that, due to standing all day, he developed excessive accumulation of serous fluid in the tissue spaces in his feet.

On one visit, a student asked if he could talk to the patient. Dr. Twerski agreed, while wondering what the young doctor could offer that had not been previously explored by the experts.

After a brief conversation the man stared blankly at the young doctor. But then the student assumed the man's exact contorted position and said to him, "I'll stand here like this. You can go sit down." The patient smiled, proceeded to a couch, and for the first time in 52 years, he actually sat down!

Dr. Twerski surmised that the patient felt he was holding up the world; without him, he felt it would collapse. (Dr. Twerski had no explanation for the meal or bedtime gaps.) The moment the patient was convinced that someone could carry the mission as well as he could, he relaxed.

Commentaries explain that the sin of the Golden Calf occurred when Moshe did not return from Sinai on time. The minute that 40 days elapsed, and Moshe was missing, the nation panicked. No one, they felt, could lead them but Moshe, so they created a false deity. And they prayed and danced to a new-found god.

The *Mishkan,* however was an antidote. Moshe charged Betzalel with the great task, and he accomplished it. In fact, our Sages explain that he even challenged Moshe in certain directives, and Hashem concurred with Betzalel! So Betzalel did indeed do what Hashem wanted — exactly the way it was told to Moshe. But Betzalel had the ability to perform as if he received the directive himself! That is the goal of *mesorah.* Although the proverbial torch is actually passed from previous leaders, tradition has the next generation holding it as if it were passed from the Almighty Himself. Through Betzalel and the *Mishkan,* the nation saw that it is possible to continue without the former leader holding up the world every step of the way. Indeed, there is room for young leadership to carry on the directives of the elder generation. That is the way the Torah continues — and thrives. And that is the way we hold up the world.

ספר ויקרא

The Book of *Leviticus*

PARSHAS VAYIKRA

Selfless Sacrifice

The beginning portions of the Book of *Vayikra* teach us the laws of sacrifices. The Jewish People have not observed such rites in 2,000 years, and comprehending the meaning and symbolism of sacrifices is perhaps as difficult as attaining proficiency in their complex laws and details. Obviously, such ideas — underlying decrees that have not been observed since the destruction of the *Bais HaMikdash* — are difficult to comprehend. As such, the offerings of animals, flour and oil mixtures, birds, and spices upon an altar are spheres above the psyche of any twentieth-century thinker.

Indeed, such deep thoughts are beyond the scope of this book: homiletic *drashos* are not the forum to expound such deep symbolism and ritual. More to the point, tomes have been written by the greatest thinkers in Jewish history in an attempt to explicate God's lofty directives for those esoteric rituals.

Yet despite space limitations, and a fundamental inability to comprehend fully such complex, mystical yet meaningful sacrificial services, we must understand one basic fact: the absolution of sin was not complete without offering some corporeal item — substituting for the mortal who should have been taken instead — through the service agency of the *kohanim* to Hashem.

The opening words of the Book of *Vayikra,* the *Toras Kohanim,* has Moshe command the nation, "When an *adam* — a man — from among you brings an offering to Hashem" *(Leviticus 1:2).* The Torah then proceeds with the hows, whens, wheres, and whos of the *korbonos.* But as the commentaries extrapolate upon every syllable, the opening verse receives as much scrutiny as the ensuing intricacies.

"When an *adam* from among you brings an offering to Hashem." In this verse, the word used for man is not the normally used *ish*, but rather *adam* — surely a reference to the original Adam, that solitary, lonely being who once dwelled in the Garden of Eden. The words "from among you" also raise a question. Isn't every individual "from among you"? Why doesn't the Torah begin its remarks, "when one offers a sacrifice"? Why the symbolic juxtaposition of *adam* and "among you"?

The rabbi was preaching to a packed crowd, and the mood was somber and tense as he expounded on the gravity of sin. Exhorting the people to repent —to do *teshuva,* he called upon them to come back to the faith and laws of their Creator. Although he was reluctant to use the power of certain words, he knew that they would stir his audience. So he added the clincher.

"Does everyone in this community know what is going to happen to them?" he asked. "Everyone in this community is going to die!"

The audience gasped in fear, and the sobriety of the moment was etched in deep creases on their faces.

All of them felt that way — except for one elderly gentleman who sat smiling in the second row directly in front of the rabbi. As the rabbi began to speak again, the man actually chuckled. Disturbed, the rabbi stopped. Perhaps the old-timer did not get the point. In even louder tones the rabbi implored, "It is time to repent!" Then he added with increased fervor, "Did you hear me? Everyone in this community is going to die!"

The man's smile broadened. Oblivious to the countenance of his fellow listeners, it was as if the rabbi's words simply had no effect on him.

The rabbi stared directly at the man, and with passion in his voice, he asked,"What's the matter with you? Don't you realize that everyone in this community is going to die?"

The old man looked back, his smile broader than ever. "Heh heh!" he chuckled. "It's all right, rabbi, I'm not from this community!"

The Torah tells us the secret of sacrifices long before it details the actual offerings. "When an *adam* will sacrifice from among you," there are no islands, and there are no individuals. Every sacrifice comes "from among you." The juxtaposition of the contrasting words — Adam, the sole creation from whom humanity descended; and *mikem,* from among you, the great mass of humanity that forms *Klal Yisrael* — are forever inseparable. Everyone, therefore, both represents community and influences it as well: and every action, whether of benevolence, charity, or sacrifice, causes ripples throughout the *klal.*

The Torah precedes the laws and details of the individual who offers a sacrifice upon the altar of the Almighty with "*adam* from amongst you." Because no *adam* emerges from emptiness, and no action is ever performed in solitude. As such, each *adam* today lives not as the sole occupant of an empty Garden of Eden. Instead, we are all clearly part of the greater community, and everything we do comes from, and affects, others who are among us.

Parshas Tzav

Room for a Broom

This portion begins as Hashem told Moshe to teach Ahron and his children a few laws. Hashem did not tell Moshe to speak to Ahron, and He did not even tell Moshe to teach Ahron. He told Moshe *"Tzav es Ahron"* — Command Ahron.

"Tzav," Rashi explains, "is a very powerful word. It means command with a charge that is to be executed with speed and diligence. The word *tzav* is also used only for situations that have eternal ramifications." Yet if we analyze the next few commands, we may be left wondering: why do those charges needed the powerful preface, *"tzav"*?

The succeeding verse is about the *korban olah,* a sacrifice that is committed entirely to Hashem: no part of the animal, save the skin, is left for human benefit or consumption. Given this sacrifice's high spiritual status, it would seem that the *tzav* is appropriate: the person who brings it would naturally want to make certain that the *korban olah* is offered according to the highest standards of *halacha*. However, the Torah only spends one verse on the *olah* before proceeding to discuss the daily task of cleaning the ashes off the altar. For that task, the Torah tells us, a *kohen* must wear linen vestments, remove the ashes, and place them near the altar.

Certainly, simple logic would dictate that such cleaning must be done. But why is this menial job mentioned together with the holy *olah*? To what end does it, too, merit the powerful command *"tzav"*?

The Steipler Gaon, Rabbi Yisrael Yaakov Kanievski, of blessed memory, was a paragon of holi-

ness. Indeed, numerous stories about his sacred inviolability are well known throughout the Torah community. At seventeen, for example, he had already survived the Russian army without compromising *Shabbos* or *kashrus*.

In addition to his many superior character traits, the Steipler was not known for lengthy conversations — due in no small part to the fact that he had lost his hearing in the Czar's army when he served as a sentry on freezing Siberian nights. Indeed, it was common practice for people to write him questions or requests to pray on behalf of the sick or unfortunate. The Steipler would read the note, hardly lift his eyes from the large volume on his old table, and would respond. If prayer were requested, he started to pray. If an *halachic* or *hashkafic* question were asked, he would often condense his answer or advice into one or two potent sentences.

People asked, he gave answers — and often within days miraculous salvation came. And so did more people, standing in lines outside his modest home. And without fail, the very old Sage would find the time to see anyone who walked in with the problems of the world bearing down on their shoulders.

One time, an aspiring young man, whose goal was to be as great a scholar as the Steipler himself, came with a problem. The young man felt that a particular predicament was impeding his spiritual growth — and surely a man like Rabbi Kanievski, who persevered in the face of life-threatening problems, could relate to this!

The young man had written the situation in detail for the Steipler so that he could grasp its severity. "Every Friday," the young man wrote, "I come home from yeshiva, and the scene in the house leads me to despair. The table is not set, the kitchen is hardly clean, and the children are not bathed! What should I do? How can I concentrate on my studies when I have such problems?" As he waited for the answer, the aspiring scholar expected the Steipler to advise him

how to deal with a wife who was not living up to his standards.

The Steipler looked up from the paper and made a grave face. The young man smiled, for he understood that the Steipler must have realized the severity of his situation. Then the Sage spoke in his heavy Russian-accented Yiddish. "You really want to know what to do?"

The young man nodded eagerly.

The Steipler looked austere.

"Take a broom!"

Rabbeinu Yonah of Girondi explains the juxtaposition of the command to sweep ashes with that of the *korban olah.* A person must realize that sometimes what is considered menial work in human eyes merits the highest accord in Hashem's eyes. That's why the *mitzvah* of sweeping the altar is prefaced with the word *tzav* and placed next to the *korban olah* —so that one will realize that the little, unglorified acts also yield great spiritual sanctity. Therefore, in the quest for spirituality, one must never demean the simple chores. For no matter how holy one is, there is always room for a broom.

PARSHAS SHEMINI

Etiquette & Candor

In teaching the kosher laws in this *parsha,* the Torah deviates from something it had done in a previous portion. Normally, the Torah does not elaborate unnecessarily, yet elsewhere it deviates from its normal propensity to abbreviate. As Rabbi Yehoshua ben Levi points out in *Tractate Pesachim,* in *Parshas Noach* the Torah adds extra words for a very special reason. "A person should never emit a harsh expression from his mouth," Rabbi Yehoshua explains. "That is why in *Parshas Noach,* when the Torah tells us that Noach brought animals into his ark, it takes pain to add extra words." There, the Torah tells us that "Noach took sets of seven males and females of each of the *tahor* species, and a set of two animals of the non-*tahor* species" (*Genesis 7:2).*

"The Torah," Rabbi Yehoshua continues, "could have used just one simple word to describe the non-kosher animals —*tamei!* Yet to teach us the importance of clean speech, the Torah uses an elaborate Hebrew terminology, calling them "animals that are not *tahor,*" instead of a simpler and shorter expression, *treif* animals. Indeed, the Torah avoids calling creatures — even non-kosher ones — *tamei;* rather, it labels them "animals that are not classified as *tahor."*

In *Parshas Shemini,* the Torah prescribes the laws of kosher and non-kosher. It specifies for us those signs and characteristics of kosher animals — and those animals, which do not meet the specifications, are deemed *tamei.* Among those classified as non-kosher are the hare, camel, hyrax, and, of course, the ubiquitous symbol of non-kosher, the pig. Waiving the graciousness of *Parshas Noach,* the Torah refers to these animals as *tamei!* The Torah does not label them "animals that are not *tahor."* It calls them *treif!* Why the curt classification here? What happened to the gentle etiquette so beautifully explicated by Rabbi Yehoshua?

The governor of a group of small villages decided to make an official visit to one of the more backward farm communities of his province. The mayor of the village, a simple farmer, who had no idea of either social graces or required etiquette, received him. The farmer's wife made tea, the water of which was scooped from a muddy stream and set to boil. Upon sipping the first bit of the dirt-filled libation, the governor immediately spit it out and shouted, "What did you serve me? This is terrible!" The governor proceeded to show the mayor and his wife how to strain water through cheesecloth in order to make a proper glass of tea. Amazed, both husband and wife accepted the advice gratefully.

A few weeks later, there was a fire in the village. Reports to the governor said that though there had been ample water, manpower, and time to contain the blaze, for some reason the fire had managed to destroy most of the town. The governor arrived at the home of the mayor to inquire what exactly went wrong.

"You see, dear governor," the hapless mayor beamed, "the men were going to use the muddy brook water to extinguished the blaze, but I stopped them! I showed them how to filter the water, and remove the small rocks and dirt. Since your visit, we have never used filthy water again!"

"You fool!" shouted the governor. "You filter for tea, not for a fire! When a fire is raging, you must put it out immediately, even with dirty water!"

Since the story of Noach is a narrative, the Torah can well afford to classify the non-kosher animals in a positive light. After all, for the sake of the story it does not make a difference if the animals are referred to as *tamei,* or as not-*tahor*. In that narrative, the Torah chose the gentler way. However, when telling us to avoid eating animals that are not kosher, the Torah does not offer circuitous etiquette, it boldly warns us "they are *treif!*"

We live in a world that is fraught with many dangers. Sometimes we must say "no" to our friends, our children, even ourselves, in a very curt and abrupt way. A particular substance, action, behavior, or influence may be much worse than "not-so-good." It may be dangerous, and must be stated as such. Saying "no," "poison," and even *"treif"* may lack the social graces, but such forcefulness may well be more effective than saying, "it's not the proper action."

There is a time and place for every expression. Most always, etiquette must be employed; but when a fire is raging, and the situation demands powerful exhortation, any water, even if it is a little muddy, must be used!

Parshas Tazria

Holistic Healing

Tzora'as, the main topic of the portions of *Tazria* and *Metzora,* is an affliction that discolors human skin, clothing, hair, beards, and even homes. Further, the laws of *tzora'as* are detailed, complex, and intricate. Indeed, there are entire Talmudic tractates dealing with the proper purification procedures, and a litany of laws must be followed flawlessly for success. Yet the ramifications of *tzora'as* have more than physiological implications: they have great theological import as well.

With *tzora'as,* the skin discoloration does not necessarily reflect a chemical impurity or a nutritional deficiency. Instead, the blemish is a heavenly sign of a spiritual flaw, primarily related to the sin of slander. The afflicted person must go to a *kohen,* who instructs him in the proper procedure to be rid of both the discoloration as well as the improper behavior that brought about its appearance.

The Torah further states that the fate of the stricken person is completely dependent upon the will of the *kohen.* Indeed, the *kohen* is shown the *negah,* and he has the power to declare it *tamei* or *tahor.* In fact, even if all signs point to a declaration of impurity, if the *kohen,* for any reason, deems the person *tahor,* or refuses to declare him *tamei,* the person remains *tahor.* The final judgment with *tzora'as* is that no one is *tamei* until openly and clearly labeled as such by a *kohen.*

Yet the verse outlining this procedure seems a bit redundant. "And the *kohen* shall look at the *negah* affliction on the skin, and, behold, it has changed to white and appears deeper than the skin of the flesh — it is a *tzora'as,* and the *kohen* shall look at him and declare him *tamei"* (*Leviticus 13:3*). Why must the *kohen* look twice? The Torah should tell us that the *kohen* shall look at the *negah,* and if the affliction is white and appears deeper than the flesh of the skin, then the *kohen* shall declare him impure. What purpose is served by looking again?

Rabbi Abraham Twerski tells the story of a young man who came to the Chief Rabbi of Vilna, Rabbi Chaim Ozer Grodzinsky, with a request. Since this young man's father was applying for a rabbinical position in a town with which the Sage was familiar, the son asked the great rabbi for a letter of approbation on his father's behalf.

Unbeknownst to the young man, Rabbi Grodzinsky felt that the candidate was not worthy of the position. Nevertheless, instead of flatly refusing, he just said that he would rather not mix into the rabbinical affairs of another city but was certain that the council of that city would make a fair and wise decision.

Unfortunately, Rabbi Grodzinsky did not realize the tirade that would be forthcoming. As the young man spewed insults at him, the Sage accepted them in silence. After a few minutes of hearing abusive language, Rabbi Grodzinsky excused himself and left the room.

Students who witnessed the barrage were shocked at the young man's audacity. They were even more surprised that the Rav did not silence the young man at the start of the barrage. Rabbi Grodzinsky turned to them. "You cannot view that onslaught on its own," he said. "You must look at the bigger picture. This young man was defending the honor of his father, and in that vein I had to overlook his lapse."

The *kohen,* who is instructed to deal with a stricken individual, should not only look at the *negah.* He must look again — at the man. Rabbi Meir Simcha HaKohen of Dvinsk explains that even if the *negah* has all the attributes that should lead to a certain declaration of *tumah,* there are other factors that must be weighed. If the man is a groom about to wed, impurity must not be declared, for it will ruin the upcoming festivities. If there are other mitigating circumstances, then a declaration of impurity must be postponed.

Perhaps the Torah is telling us more. It is easy to look at a flaw and declare it as such. But one must look at the whole person. One must ask oneself, "How will my declaration affect the future of this person?" One must consider the circumstances that caused the *negah.* Then one must look again — once at the *negah,* and once at the man.

There are those who interpret the adage in *Pirkei Avos* (Ethics of the Fathers), "judge all people in a good way," as an instruction not to just look merely at part of a person. Rather, judge *all* of the person — for even an obvious flaw may have a motivation or rationale behind it. The *kohen* may look at the *negah,* but before he pronounces *tamei* he must look again. He must look beyond the blemish. He must look at the man.

Parshas Metzora

Self-Help

In defining the laws of *tzora'as,* the disease that affects people with a white skin blemish, the Torah outlines a detailed process by which the affliction is contracted, diagnosed, and cured. The afflicted, one who has contracted *tzora'as,* is referred to as a *metzora,* and the Talmud tells us that the disease comes from the sin of slander. As soon as the potential *metzora* notices a discoloration of the skin, he must immediately visit a *kohen* for spiritual counsel. By Torah law, the *kohen* is the only one who is able to declare a state of impurity by officially acknowledging the disease, to dismiss the initial diagnosis, or to announce the successful recuperation. Of course, one who has indulged in the evils of scandalous gossip would be well served by a priest, and it is indeed the *kohen* who guides the *metzora* through the healing process.

If, after an incubation period that follows the initial observation, the *tzora'as* subsides, the afflicted patient is declared *tahor* and may return to the camp from which he had been previously expelled.

In this portion, the Torah reviews the healing process, which involves, among other rites, sacrificial offerings and immersion in a *mikveh.* But before any of this is done, the Torah tells us that the "*kohen* shall go to the outside of the camp and shall look (at the afflicted one), and, behold, the *tzara'as* affliction has been healed from the *metzora*" (*Leviticus 14:3*).

A number of commentators are intrigued by the Torah's extra verbiage. It would have been enough to state, "and behold the *tzara'as* affliction has been healed." Why must the Torah add the words, "from the afflicted *metzora*"? Of course, the blemish was healed "from the *metzora*." Surely it was not the *kohen* who was healed!

A fellow decided to go out drinking after work. At 2 a.m., the bar closed, and he went home drunk.

As he tiptoed up the stairs, he tripped and fell head over heels. Landing on his face, breaking the nearly empty pint bottle that fell from his back-pocket, the broken glass cut him on his cheek and forehead, but he was so drunk he did not immediately realize that he was injured.

A few minutes later, as he was undressing, he noticed blood on his clothes, so he checked himself in the mirror. He repaired the damage as best he could under the circumstances, and he went to bed.

The next morning, his head throbbed, and his injury was painful. Hunkering under the covers, he was trying to think up a good story when his wife came into the bedroom.

"Well, you surely must have been drunk last night," she said. "I thought you promised to stop drinking!"

"I worked late," he said, "and I came home after you were asleep."

"That's a lie," she replied. "What are the cuts on your face all about?"

"Oh, I tripped on the way out of the office," the man replied, feeling the dried blood on his cheek and forehead. Then he felt for the band-aids, but there were none. Confused, he thought that he had cleaned, salved, and bandaged his wounds.

His wife laughed cynically. "You were very drunk last night, and I won't put up with it any longer!"

"What makes you so sure I got drunk last night, anyway?" he countered.

"Well," she replied, "my first big clue was when I got up this morning and found first aid cream and a bunch of band-aids stuck all over the mirror!"

Perhaps the words, "healed from the afflicted *metzora*," teach us a lesson about every affliction that stems from a spiritual malady. There is nowhere to find a cure but from within the afflicted himself. External salves are only temporary solutions that do not affect the core problem. And if they are not applied to the actual wound, they are worthless. If the issue that caused the affliction in the case of the *metzora* was immoderate and unacceptable gossip, then the remedy must come from within. There is no excuse, nowhere to place the blame but on the *metzora* himself. And the only way the blemish will heal is when the "*tzara'as* affliction has been healed from the *metzora*."

Parshas Acharei-Mos

Visitation Rites

Among the many intricacies entailed in the laws of *korbonos* is the prohibition of *shechutai chutz*. After the *Mishkan*, and later the Holy Temple, was designated as the sole place to which the Jewish people had to bring offerings, the Torah prohibited an animal sacrifice to be offered — or even slaughtered — outside these areas. From the verses in this *parsha*, it seems that one of the reasons for this prohibition was to stem the tide of idolatrous offerings that were then prevalent. The Torah commands that "Any man from the house of Israel who will slaughter a bull, a sheep, or a goat in the camp, or who will slaughter it outside the camp — and he has not brought it to the entrance of the Tent of Meeting, to bring it as an offering to Hashem before the Tabernacle of Hashem — it shall be considered as bloodshed for that man. He has shed blood, and that man shall be cut off from his people" (*Leviticus* 17:3-4).

Killing animals, then, was not an indifferent exercise. Indeed, during the sojourn in the desert, consuming meat was only permitted in conjunction with a spiritual offering — and, in fact, animals could not even be killed and offered except through an act of spirituality.

Once again, the Torah clearly states its reasoning: "So that the Children of Israel will bring their feast-offerings that they have been slaughtering on the open field, and they shall bring them to Hashem, to the entrance of the Tent of Meeting, to the *kohen*; and they shall slaughter them as feast peace-offerings to Hashem" (*Leviticus* 17:5).

Moreover, the Torah exhorts: "They shall no longer slaughter their offerings to the demons after whom they stray;

this shall be an eternal decree to them for their generations" (*Leviticus 17:7*).

If it seems that this law is also meant to stop demonic rites, why does the Torah keep mentioning that the Jewish people should bring their offerings to the sanctuary and the *kohen*? In fact, in the Temple era, a *kohen* did not necessarily slaughter the animal; instead, he began his service after the *shechita*. (Rav Zalman of Volozhin noted that unlike in the era of the *Bais Hamikdash,* in which an Israelite was allowed to do the slaughtering, in the era of the Wilderness Generation the *kohen* was indeed required to slaughter the animals.)

We are left, then, with a conundrum. Not even the most pious Jew, one who would surely not worship idols, demons, or spirits, was allowed to conduct his spiritual rites outside the *Mikdash*. Why?

There is a wonderful story about the Gerrer Rebbe, Rabbi Simcha Bunim Alter, of blessed memory, known to thousands of *chasidim* as the *Laiv Simcha*.

One of the Gerrer Rebbe's more prosperous followers had opened a new store to which he devoted quite a bit of time. Unfortunately, within months of the grand opening, his original business began to falter badly. After a few futile back-office manipulations, he decided to go to the Rebbe for a blessing.

The Rebbe thought a few moments and then asked where the man's office was.

"It is in my new spacious headquarters," the man said proudly.

The Rebbe then told the man that each day after 10:00 AM he should kiss the *mezuzah* of his old store a number of times.

The advice sounded more mystical than practical, but as a faithful follower the man complied. Each day after 10:00, he drove to his old location and kissed the *mezuzah*.

Surprisingly, within two months sales were booming, and the store had resumed its success.

The man returned to the Rebbe filled with gratitude and wonder. "Please tell me what type of *segulah* (meritorious act) was that?" he asked. "Why did kissing my *mezuzah* help turn the business around?"

The Rebbe explained. " The truth is that kissing the *mezuzah* did not turn the business around. You did. You see, ever since you opened the new store, I assumed that you neglected to visit your first store. The employees slacked off, and the enthusiasm was not there. But I could not tell you that. After all, I am a Rebbe. Who am I to tell an accomplished businessmen which business to nurture?

"However, by telling you to kiss the *mezuzah,* I knew that you would go to the store. Once you were there, you would make sure that whatever had to be done, was done!"

True, the *kohen* does not slaughter. True, a man can pursue spirituality on open plains. But the Torah reveals a secret in attaining the true goal of holiness. Visit the place of spiritual business. It is rare that one can attain success in his quest for spirituality by doing it on his own; and though he may not be slaughtering to demons, he surely can misconstrue Hashem's intentions. To rephrase the inimitable words of President Calvin Coolidge, the business of Judaism is spiritual business. And the Torah tells us that the place of spiritual business is the *Mikdash*!

Parshas Kedoshim

Limited Partnership

Respect for one's parents is a universal concept, as universal as a day of rest. And in the portion of *Kedoshim* both concepts are taught in a single verse. "Every man: Your mother and father you shall revere, and My *Shabbos* you shall observe, I am Hashem, your God" (*Leviticus 19:3*). Two commandments, the Sabbath and parental honor are placed together. Yet they are not only juxtaposed for their universality or importance; indeed, the Talmud derives an important *halachic* ruling from the positioning. The Talmud explains that the honor of parents only goes up to a point: it may not override Torah observance. Thus, if parents command a child to desecrate a Torah law, such as the observance of *Shabbos*, the child is no longer commanded to heed them. Therefore, the caveat of *Shabbos* is clearly understood in relationship to parental obedience.

The words that follow, however, seem superfluous. "I am Hashem, your God." Why did the Torah add that? Those words, "I am Hashem, your God," are usually placed in conjunction with commandments that deal with secret intentions: cheating, lying, falsifying weights and measures, and so on. Those are instances where the victim is fooled — and only Hashem knows the truth. In *Deuteronomy*, for example, the Torah admonishes us to keep proper weights and measures, then adds, "I am Hashem." Dishonoring parents seems different. The victims are well aware of the sin of disrespect. After all, they are the clear recipients of the disrespect. Why, then, must the Torah add "I am Hashem" in relationship to parental honor? Could the Torah be giving us a new perspective of parental honor?

An old man, sitting on a Central Park bench on a sweltering August day, noticed two workers getting off a truck parked on the lawn. Each had a shovel in his hand, and a variety of gardening tools were strapped to the heavy leather belts that held up their thick, grass-stained dungarees. The workers surveyed the area. Then, as if on cue, one of them began to dig furiously. He dug and dug, while the other worker looked on, almost indifferently. Finally, the digger lifted his sweaty head from the ground and smiled. He had opened a large hole by his feet. Then the two workers looked at each other, stood back, and waited. Nothing, however, was happening. After about ten minutes, the first fellow glanced at his watch, shrugged his shoulders, and nodded to the second man.

As if on cue, the second fellow began filling the hole with the earth that was just removed. He patted the filled hole firmly and nodded to the first fellow, who nodded back his approval. With smug smiles of great accomplishment, they walked about 12 feet from their first location and began the procedure again. While the filler watched, the digger dug a hole. Upon its completion, he stopped. Then both workers waited exactly 10 minutes. The nod came, and while the first fellow watched, the second fellow repacked the hole until it was firm and neat.

After six repetitions of the bizarre episode, the elderly man on the bench could no longer contain himself. "What in the world are you guys doing?" he exclaimed. "What have you accomplished? Are you digging or filling? What's going on here?"

"Take it easy!" boomed the first worker. "We're planting trees here! I dig the hole, then the next guy puts the tree in, and finally, him, over here," he said pointing to the second worker, "fills the hole and packs it real neat. This way the tree has strong support."

Before the elderly gentleman could open his mouth, the second fellow chimed in. "We're union workers, and the guy who plants the trees didn't show up today! But we are here doin' our jobs. Cause, oh no! We ain't missin' a day's pay 'cause he didn't show!"

The Torah tells us that there is more to honoring parents than a commitment only to the people themselves. There is another partner who must always be taken into account: "I am Hashem." Fear and respect of parents are an integral part of the equation. Nevertheless, without affording the proper recognition to the Creator, it's as if one were digging a hole, and filling it, without planting the tree. There is an underlying meaning to the fact that *mitzvos* supercede the laws of respect: the third partner holds the key to the first two. And without Hashem, we can dig and fill but, at the end of the day, there will be no fruit to show for our efforts.

Parshas Emor

Holier than Thou

One of the most disheartening episodes that occurred during the 40-year desert sojourn is recorded in this portion. A man quarreled with a fellow Jew and left the dispute in a rage. He then compounded his sin by blaspheming Hashem. This abhorrent behavior was so aberrant that no one even knew what the punishment was!

So Hashem expounded the punishment for this deplorable act. As in any society, the ultimate act of treason was met with a capital sentence. Accordingly, the Torah declared the death penalty. But curiously enough, Hashem did not leave it at that. When the Torah reveals the penalty for the heinous act of blasphemy, it continues:

"And one who blasphemes the name of Hashem shall be put to death…And if a man inflicts a mortal wound in his fellow man, he shall be put to death. If he inflicts damage, then restitution shall be paid. The value of a break for a break; the value of an eye for the loss of an eye; the value of a tooth for the loss of a tooth. And one who wounds an animal must be made to pay (*Leviticus* 24:15-21).

Why lump blasphemy in with these more petty injuries? Shouldn't the greater crime be in a league of its own? Surely the act of affronting God Almighty cannot be equated with attacking human beings. And surely it has no place next to the laws of injurious action towards animals!

Rabbi Y'honasan Eibeschutz, one of Jewry's most influential rabbinical leaders during the early 1700s, was away from his home for one Yom Kippur and was

forced to spend that holy day in a small town. Without revealing his identity, he entered the synagogue towards evening and surveyed the room, looking for a suitable place to sit and pray.

Toward the center of the synagogue, his eyes fell upon a man who was swaying fervently, tears welling in his eyes. "How encouraging," the Rabbi thought. "I will sit next to him. His prayers will surely inspire me."

The man cried softly as he prayed, tears flowing down his face. "I am but dust in my life, oh Lord," wept the man. "Surely in death!" The sincerity was indisputable. Reb Y'honasan finished his prayers that evening truly inspired. The next morning, he took his seat next to the man, who, once again, poured out his heart to God, declaring his insignificance and lack of merit.

Everything continued wonderfully, except during the congregation's reading of the Torah, something amazing happened. A man from the front of the synagogue was called for the third *aliyah*, one of the most honorable *aliyos* for an Israelite, and suddenly Rabbi Eibeschutz's neighbor charged the podium!

"Him!" the man shouted. "You give him *shlishi*?!" The *shul* went silent, and Reb Y'honasan stared in disbelief. "Why, I know how to learn three times as well as he! I give more charity than he, and I have a more illustrious family! Why on earth would you give him an *aliyah* over me?"

With that, the man stormed back from the *bimah* toward his seat.

Rabbi Eibeschutz could not believe what he saw and was forced to approach the man. "I don't undertand," he began. "Minutes ago, you were crying about how insignificant and unworthy you are, and now you are clamoring to get the honor of that man's *aliyah?"*

Disgusted, the man snapped back. "What are you talking about? Compared to Hashem I am truly a nothing." Then he pointed to the *bimah* and sneered. "But not compared to him!"

Perhaps the Torah deliberately reiterates the laws of damaging mortals and animals in direct conjunction with the directives about blasphemy. Often, people are very careful about the honor they bestow on their spiritual guides, mentors, and institutions. More so, they are scrupulous about the reverence and esteem they accord their Creator. But mortal feelings, property, and possessions are frequently trampled upon — even harmed — by those who seem to have utmost respect for the immortal.

In this portion, the Torah, after declaring the enormity of blasphemy, does not forget to mention the iniquity of striking someone less than Omnipotent. Further, the Torah links the anthropomorphic blaspheming of God to the crime of physical damage meted against those created in His image. The Torah places all these crimes next to each other because *all* of Hashem's creations must be treated with respect. Starting from the animals and reaching to the Almighty.

Parshas Behar

Ask Me No Questions...

The Torah does not usually leave room for official questions of faith. It tells us, in no uncertain terms, what our responsibilities are, and the commitment we must make to be observant Jews. Every *mitzvah* entails sacrifice. Sometimes, fulfilling a *mitzvah* requires a commitment of money, sometimes a commitment of time and morals. Not often does the Torah consider the human trials one encounters in *mitzvah* performance. Indeed, such difficulties are our problem, and we must deal with them as human beings and as Jews.

Yet in this *parsha,* the Torah uncharacteristically provides leeway for those who may waver in their commitment to do a *mitzvah.*

In *Parshas Behar,* the Torah charges the Jewish people with the laws of *shmittah.* Every seventh year, we are told, the land of Israel is to lie fallow; no work is to be done with the earth. There is not to be a harvest, nor may the ground be sown or reaped.

Observing *shmittah* is a true test of faith. Imagine! One must not harvest his grain but instead rely on pure faith for his daily fare. Yet the Torah does not leave us with this austere command. Instead, it deals directly with the human emotion related to the issue. "And if you will say [in your heart], 'what shall we eat in the seventh year, behold the land has not been sown nor has it been reaped?'" (*Leviticus 25:20*). Hashem then reassures the people that His bounty will abound in the sixth year, and during the seventh year they will live in comfort.

Shmittah is not the only time the Torah recognizes human wariness. In reference to the command of conquering the land of Canaan, the Torah tells us, "Perhaps you shall say in your heart, 'these nations are more numerous than me. How will I drive them out?'"(*Deuteronomy 7:17*) Once again, Hashem reassures His nation that He will not forsake them.

The question is glaring. Why does the Torah answer the human psyche? Why doesn't the Torah just command us to let the land lie fallow, or conquer the land of Canaan? If there are problems or fears in our hearts, they are *our* problems — not God's. As such, those fears should not be incorporated as part of *His* commands —or should they?

Isidore met his friend Irving every other week while doing business. "How are you, Irving?" Isidore always asked. "How's the wife and kids?"

Irv always grunted back the perfunctory replies. "Fine." "A little under the weather." "My son Jack got a job."

This one-sided interrogation went on for years until one day Isidore exploded. "Irv," he said abruptly. "I don't understand. For six years, I ask you about your wife, your kids, and your business. Not once, mind you, not once did you ever ask me about my wife, my kids, or my business!"

Irv shrugged. "Sorry, Izzie. I was really selfish. So tell me," he continued, "how is your wife? How are your kids? How is your business?"

Izzie let out a sigh of anguish and began to *krechts*. He put his hand gently on Irv's shoulder, tightened his lips, and shook his head slowly. "Don't ask!" he replied.

Rabbi Leible Eiger explains that there are many questions of faith that we may have. Even the faithful may fear the fact that there is fear. "Is it a flaw in faith to worry?" "Am I committing heresy by fearing the enemy?" "Am I allowed to ask?"

So the Torah tells us in two places, "You will have these questions. You will ask, 'how am I going to sustain myself and family?' You will worry, 'how will I conquer my enemies? Will I be destroyed?'" The Torah then reassures us that there is no lack of trust by asking such questions. We mustn't get down on ourselves and consider those questions a breach of faith. Life and sustenance are mortal attributes. They warrant mortal fear.

Adam, the first man, was originally blessed with eternal life without having to worry about his livelihood. After sinning, he was cursed with death and was told that he would eat by the sweat of his brow. The Torah then assures us that it is not only human but acceptable to worry about these two issues — livelihood and survival. Indeed, we can be concerned — just as long as we believe in the reassurances about our worries.

Parshas Bechukosai

Hiding From No One

This *parsha* contains the *Tochaha,* a series of unimaginable curses that, with prescient clarity, foretold the horrors that were destined to befall our people in our wanderings in exile.

Consider the barbarity of the Inquisition, the cruelty of the Crusades, and the horrors of the Holocaust: they all reflect the Torah's stern admonitions, the fate of a wayward nation cast out from the land of its inheritance. The *parsha* also tells of the destruction of cities and the starvation of their citizens. One of the curses is even about running from our enemies. "And you shall run the flight of one who flees from a sword, yet no one is pursuing you" *(Leviticus 26:36*). Simply explained, the Torah is telling us of the inherent fear that is the residue of the suffering we have endured. We shall run at the slightest thought — even when there is no one in pursuit.

The question arises: Is it not better to run from a figment of the imagination than have to flee from an actual pursuer? All in all, the imagination cannot brandish a weapon!

Al Feurstein is a retired businessman who volunteers in our yeshiva's financial office. More than that, he is a Holocaust survivor who recently told the story of his ordeals in the concentration camps and death marches that may have wracked his 16-year-old body but were unable to conquer his faith and conviction.

After enduring years of unspeakable horrors, the war ended, and Al arrived in the United States. With the help of relatives, he resettled in Laurelton, New

York. A few weeks after his arrival, he was invited to speak at his cousin's synagogue.

As he recounted his personal story, detailing the atrocities perpetrated by the Nazis and their willing civilian executioners, mouths fell open in literal disbelief. News had reached the United States of mass murders and barbarism, but never had these congregants heard in full detail how human beings could perform such horrific crimes.

What happened after his first talk so many years ago was most depressing, compounding manyfold the terror of his experiences. A few prominent members of the congregation approached him. "Al, my dear boy," they coddled him. "You couldn't have seen and experienced those tales you told! We are sure you are shell-shocked from the terrible hardships you endured. After all, it could not have been all that bad."

The worst curse may actually be when no one believes that another's calamities have happened. Perhaps that idea is also included in the curse "no one shall pursue you."

A great *Rosh Yeshiva* was complaining bitterly about not feeling well. Some colleagues did not take him seriously at first, humoring him by saying that his pains were more in his mind than in his body. Before those pains were diagnosed as the disease that eventually claimed his life, the *Rosh Yeshiva* lamented: "The Talmud in *Bava Basra 15a* debates the historical timeframe of the story of Iyov (Job). Some say he lived during the time of Moshe, others maintain he lived during the period of the Judges, and yet others even claim that he lived during the period of Purim. However, there is one opinion that Iyov never existed at all, and the entire episode is only a parable."

Painfully, the *Rosh Yeshiva* commented, "That opinion was Iyov's worst nightmare. Imagine, after all the pain and suffering Iyov endured, there is an opinion that he did not even exist!"

Perhaps in this portion, the Torah alludes to another form of curse. When there is pain and suffering, when there is persecution and oppression, yet the world ignores the cries of those suffering — it is as if "no one is pursuing" and that is a terrible curse, too. Perhaps that curse is as difficult as when the aggressors are clearly recognized for who they are. Because often our greatest enemies are not recognized as such: we are told that they are our partners, and our fears are nothing but paranoia. Even now, deniers, scoffers, and skeptics are discrediting our recent appalling ordeals.

We cannot control the ears and tongues of our detractors, but we can do our utmost to tell our stories and make sure that they live on. And we can do our best to hear, too, the pain and suffering of those who cry to us, and make sure we understand the pursuers behind the pain.

ספר במדבר

The Book of Numbers

Parshas Bamidbar

Background Checkout

The Book of *Numbers* begins with the Torah's command to take a census of the Jewish nation. From every tribe, each male over 20 was to be counted. However, the tribe of Levi was singled out to remain uncounted in the national census: "You shall not count the tribe of Levi, and you shall not take a census of them from among the Children of Israel" (*Numbers 1:49*). Levi was indeed counted, but separately and differently: the children were counted from one-month-old as opposed to 20-years-old. They were counted at a separate occasion, and their numbers were not included in the national census.

Why did Levi merit such distinctive treatment? The *Midrash* states that Hashem specially designated *shevet* Levi to be considered as the King's special legions. Why? In the midst of the sin of the Golden Calf, when so many of their fellow Jews served the idol, the tribe of Levi was stalwart in its opposition to the pagan rite. Therefore, when Levi displayed its loyalty by not worshiping the calf, it was chosen to serve in the Temple in the place of the firstborns, who were originally designated to perform the service. The *Midrash* quotes the Almighty: "The Levites made themselves close to Me, and I will be close to them."

The *Chidushei HaRim*, Rabbi Yisrael Meir Alter of Gur, asks an important question. "Surely," he writes, "there were some Jews who did not serve the Golden Calf. Why, then, was Levi singled out to serve in the *Mishkan*? Why didn't Hashem select everyone who did not serve the Golden Calf?"

In the late 1950s, not too long after Nikita Khrushchev's rise to power in the former Soviet

Union, he addressed a large gathering of the communist faithful. Beginning by excoriating the crimes and misdeeds of his predecessor, Joseph Stalin, Khrushchev promised a new era of freedom and civility. Yet as he was decrying the purges, crackdowns, and horrific crimes of his predecessor, a meek voice called out from the back of the room.

"Mr. Chairman," a man asked, "why didn't you say something? "Where were you when all this was happening?"

It was apparent that Khrushchev heard the question. His face turned red as he retorted in a menacing voice, "Who said that?"

There was silence.

The new Premier screamed louder. "Who is the one who asked where I was? I want to see him now!"

A stillness filled the room. No one moved.

Then a sly smile spread over Khrushchev's face. He looked toward the back of the large room. In slow and calculated staccato spurts he began to shout, "I know exactly where you are! I know exactly where you are standing!"

The nervous silence was unbearable, as the large audience awaited the fate of the poor man.

"I know where you are standing," repeated the feared leader of the world's largest communist country.

"You are standing in the exact spot where I stood when Stalin used to make his speeches!"

The *Chidushei HaRim* explains that there was a great difference between the passive resistance of Jews who did not serve the idol and the tribe of Levi who did much more. Because when Moshe cried, "Whoever is on the side of Hashem join with me!" the only collective group which responded was Levi, who battled the blasphemers with courageous conviction.

Many Jews may have refrained from worshipping the calf, the Rebbe of Gur explains, but only those who stood up and protested deserved to direct the spirituality of the nation. While silence may sometimes remove the burden of culpability, it can never crown one with the strength of leadership.

Parshas Naso

Pennies from Heaven

The portion of *Naso* contains the phrases that are said everyday by every congregation in the world. In the Diaspora, they are incorporated in the *chazzan*'s repetition of the *Shemoneh Esrei*, the *Amidah*, and in Israel the *kohanim* themselves recite them each morning as they bless the nation with *Birkas Kohanim*, the priestly blessings. Hashem instructed the *kohanim* to bless the people: "Thus shall you bless the nation of Israel; speak unto them. May Hashem bless you and safeguard you. May He illuminate His countenance upon you and let you find grace. May He lift His countenance upon you and establish peace for you" (*Numbers 6:23-26*).

It seems that we ask for more than blessing. Why is each one of the blessings followed with its practical implication? Bless us . . . and safeguard us. Illuminate us . . . and let us find favor in the eyes of others. Lift Your countenance . . . and establish peace for us. Is it not enough to be blessed and have the illumination of His countenance? What is the necessity of the second half of each blessing?

My friend Robert Harris of Woodmere told me a wonderful story:

A man once pleaded with the Almighty to bestow a bit of His abundance upon him. The fellow implored and begged his Creator for long life and wealth. After all, the poor soul figured, God had an abundance of everything: why then, wouldn't He spare something for a Jew in need? So the man

entered a huge, empty synagogue on the Lower East Side and began to cry.

"*Ribono Shel Olam*," he cried "in the great extent of Your eternity, what is a million years?"

The man began to tremble. He imagined that he actually heard a response.

"To Me a million years is just a mere second!" boomed a voice inside his mind.

The man then continued. "And," he asked, "to the magnitude of Your great bounty, what, may I ask, is a billion dollars?"

"A billion dollars is just a mere penny," came the resonating reply.

"Then," the man begged, "can I not have just one of your pennies?"

"Surely!" came the response, followed by a pause. "But first you must wait a mere second!"

It is not enough to get a blessing from Hashem. The blessing must be given with the assurance that it will have a practical implication. Indeed, many people receive blessings of wealth and health only to lose them to thieves and aggravation. So each of the priestly blessings is followed by a safeguard — a follow-up. The blessing of wealth alone is not enough: Hashem must guard it. Illuminating us with His countenance is not enough: unless fellow humans appreciate the grace that God has given the Jews, it is a worthless gift. And, of course, even if He lifts his countenance upon us, we still need the blessings of *shalom* — peace.

Here, the Torah also teaches us that blessings must be given with a full heart and a full hand. Generosity bestowed, must include a vehicle for appreciation. Otherwise, it is a gift of a billion dollars — in a million years. We may give blessings to our fellow Jews, but the greatest blessings we receive and give are those that endure — immediately and forever.

Parshas B'halos'cha

It's the Real Thing

This week's *parsha* contains a brief conversation that may get lost in the myriad details of some of its more fascinating events and commands. Moshe beseeches his father-in-law, Yisro, to continue traveling with the Jewish nation. "We are traveling to the place of which Hashem has said, 'I shall give it to you.' Go with us, and we shall treat you well" (*Numbers 10:29*).

Yisro replied by saying that he would like to return to his land and family. Moshe implored Yisro by telling him that he must accompany the Jews. After all, Yisro "knew the encampments and would be as eyes for the Jewish people" (v. 31).

Whether Yisro was influenced by his son-in-law's arguments is debated by the commentaries. The Torah does not refer to the outcome. What interests me, however, is that Moshe never tells Yisro where the Jews were going. He just told him that we are traveling to the place of which Hashem has said, "I shall give it to you."

It is almost reminiscent of Hashem commanding Avraham to travel to Canaan with the petition "go from your land and your birthplace to the land that I will show you" (*Genesis 12:1*). But Moshe is not the Almighty, and the entire nation knew of the land where they would be going. The land of Canaan was the focal point of the Exodus.

Why, then, does Moshe describe it to Yisro in a mysterious manner, not by defining its location, longitude or latitude, but rather identifying it as "the land that Hashem has promised to give us"? Would it not have been easier for Moshe to tell Yisro, "We are traveling to the land of Canaan, and we want you to accompany us"?

New York Times columnist Ralph de Toledano had a different view of the world than that of his editors. Despite protestations of the editorial board of the _Times_ he would always capitalize the words Heaven and Hell in any context.

His editors called him to task citing that heaven is only capitalized when it is an alternative for the Deity as in "Heaven help us." Moreover, they insisted that hell never got a capital H.

De Toledano, however, insisted that any reference of those two places be spelled with an initial capital letter.

"You see," the conservative columnist explained, "Heaven and Hell must always be capitalized. I want my readers to understand that Heaven and Hell are _real places_ — just like Scarsdale!"

When describing the Land of Israel, Moshe did not take a topographical approach. He delved deeper. Moshe *Rabbeinu* did not refer to the land of Israel merely as the land of Canaan. He did not even describe *Eretz Yisrael* as the land flowing with milk and honey. Moshe's only descriptive was, "the place of which Hashem has said, 'I shall give it to you.' "

That statement describes *Eretz Yisrael* in much stronger terms than expressions of agricultural potential, natural beauty, or strategic location.

It tells us that *Eretz Israel* is the place that Hashem promised us. Any other quality is temporal. Bounty withers, beauty erodes, and natural resources dry-up. But the promise of Hashem remains eternal. It makes us understand that like both extremes of the World-to-Come, the land of Israel is real.

Parshas Shelach

Lure of Life

Rarely do we find that Hashem's commands take on personal connotations. Instead, they are conferred for the sake of Judaism and the glory of Heaven. Yet, disturbingly, we find the mission of the spies defined with very personal overtones. The Torah begins here with Hashem commanding Moshe, "Send spies for yourself to scour the land of Israel" (*Numbers 13:2*). Why is the command tainted with such a personal epithet? Did Moshe send the spies for himself?

In fact, Moshe reviewed the entire episode in *Deuteronomy*, stating how the idea of spies found favor in his eyes. The commentaries are quick to point out that the idea found favor in Moshe's mortal's eyes, but Hashem disapproved. Therefore, He told Moshe send the spies for yourself. "As far as I am concerned," Hashem implies, "it is a mistake, but if sending spies is what you desire, then proceed." Thus, He uses the words, "send spies for yourself."

Of course, the dire consequences of the mission are well known. The spies returned and maligned the land of Israel. They were punished, along with the entire nation that joined them in their misconceived sorrow, and the next 40 years were spent wandering in the desert.

Yet we are human, we live in a corporeal world, and our intentions are tinged with mortal bias. Therefore, isn't every mortal action filled with human bias and mortal partiality? What then, is the message of the powerful allusion, "send spies for yourself" and not for Me?

A wealthy man decided to take up the sport of fishing. After renting a cottage near a Vermont lake,

he barreled into the local sport and wildlife shop and demanded to see the manager.

"I want to buy the best of everything: the most expensive rod and tackle, the best hooks, anglers, and even the most expensive bait!" the man exclaimed.

The store owner, who had seen his share of city-folk, was not impressed. He instructed a young salesman to follow the man around the store and serve as a human shopping cart. The man chose the most exquisite rods and reels; he selected a mahogany tackle box and a refrigerated bait cooler. Money was no object, and the fisherman-to-be selected the finest of everything. The enthusiastic young salesman was extremely eager to please and offered him every imaginable fishing item and accessory. The owner, a crusty and seasoned Vermonter, just smirked at the naivete of the new-found angler.

As the tycoon approached the checkout counter, he noticed brightly colored, hand-painted fishing lures whose prices were as outlandish as their colors. "Wow!" he exclaimed, as he gathered a bunch into his hand. "These look really wonderful!" Then he turned to the manager and in a voice sounding as well informed as possible, he asked the owner, "Do fish really go for these?"

"Don't know," shrugged the old-timer. "I don't sell to fish."

Moshe reluctantly agreed to the whims and premonitions of a nervous and anxious nation. He agreed to their pleading to allow spies to check out the land that they would ultimately inherit. But by no means was it a Divine mission. By telling Moshe to "send spies for yourself," Hashem taught Moshe that missions fueled by self-fulfillment are doomed.

Often, we stand at the check-out counter of life and choose impulse items with the view that they are necessary for our success. We marvel at the brightly-colored lures and find it hard to imagine life without them. We rationalize that they are needed for the sake of family, livelihood, even spirituality. We think we are purchasing them for lofty reasons and negate the fact that perhaps selfishness and insecurity are the driving forces behind the sale. We buy them thinking that they are the items that will catch the fish, but ultimately we are the only ones caught!

Moshe was about to send spies on a seemingly sacred mission, one that could have been falsely justified in hundreds of different ways: the operation would save lives, it would prepare a young nation for a smooth transition, it would create a new level of spirituality for the fledgling folk. But those were not the true objectives; instead, there was selfishness involved, and the mission was doomed. For the road to the lowest places is paved with disingenuous holy intent.

Therefore, Hashem told Moshe not to confuse himself, that there was only one motivation behind the mission. They were not sending spies for Hashem. Instead, the nation sent spies for its own ego and insurance. And so Hashem declared, "Send them for yourself." God does not need scouts, guides, or pathfinders. His actions are not meant to appease or cajole. While He may yield to those who are selfish, He will not sell to fish! And ultimately it is those who fool themselves that get the hook.

Parshas Korach

Grinding the Point

The sojourn in the desert was no walk in the park. True, it was a period of time in which miracles were the norm, and the level of spirituality soared, but life next to God required a perfect commitment.

The actions of the Jewish nation were scrutinized, the eyes of Hashem peering as a strict teacher, correcting and adjusting every wrong move with immediate censure and swift action. Indeed, we suffered for our mistakes. The Jews wandered for 40 years because of the erroneous reports of the spies. And the many rebellions and uprisings concerning the manna and other matters, including the ever-present desire to return to Egypt, were met with swift, decisive retribution. In this portion, however, the rebels were rebuked in three different ways, each a miracle unto itself.

Korach organized a rebellion against Moshe and Ahron. Claiming nepotistic inconsistency, Korach said that Ahron did not deserve the position of *Kohen Gadol*. After all, Korach claimed, "The entire congregation is holy. Why, then," he argued with Moshe, "do you raise yourselves higher than the rest of the congregation of the Lord?" (*Numbers 16:3*)

But that time, the punishment was no ordinary plague. First, in a display of absolute power and sovereignty, Hashem opened the earth, which swallowed Korach and his immediate family of rabble-rousers whole and alive! Then Korach's 250 co-conspirators were consumed by fire as they attempted to offer a sweet-smelling *k'tores* sacrifice.

Afterwards, to quell more grumbling, another miracle occurred. Each tribal leader was commanded to place a staff in the ground; miraculously, only Ahron's began to sprout buds before their eyes. It grew leaves, flowers, and almonds — a heavenly sign that only Ahron merited the exalted position of *Kohen Gadol*.

Now opening the earth was no little feat, for earthquakes of that magnitude did not occur at a moment's notice! Wasn't that event powerful enough to make the point? Why was there a need to quell the whining and punish the perpetrators with more powerful acts and magnificent miracles? Shouldn't the first Divine warning have been enough?

My cousin Rabbi Nussen Speigel related the following story that happened to his great-great grandfather.

Rabbi Meshulam Igra of Pressburg was one of Europe's leading scholars in the latter part of the 18th Century. As a young man, he was engaged to the daughter of a prominent community leader in the city of Butzatz. A few months before the wedding, the young groom-to-be ate a meal at the home of his future father-in-law. Dessert came with a treat Reb Meshulam, who had grown up in dire poverty, had never heard of — coffee.

The servant brought out the grinds, sugar, milk, and a carafe of boiled water. The prospective father-in-law directed his future son-in-law to partake. The young scholar looked quizzically at each of the entities and began to ponder. As more important foods receive a blessing before others, he contemplated the halachic order in which to consume them. He took a spoonful of coffee grinds, sprinkled some sugar on them, made the blessing he thought appropriate, and began to eat them. Not wanting to embarrass his soon-to-be father-in-law who had served such a difficult-to-eat dessert, he slowly chewed and swallowed the grinds. His prospective bride stood in shock. She motioned her father to a corner.

"Father," she cried "I cannot marry a man who does not know how do drink a cup of coffee. He is totally unsophisticated!" With that, the engagement was broken.

A few years later, this same community leader was visiting the home of a prominent *rav* in Hamburg, who was in the middle of reviewing a difficult question regarding the status of a marriage. It was, in fact, the issue of the day, and the rabbi had a stack of letters from all over Europe with various opinions on the matter.

Before the man began his conversation, the rabbi turned to him. "I receive much correspondence concerning this particular case," he said. "But today I received a correspondence from a brilliant young man which has opened my eyes in an entirely new way. In fact, I do not think a man of this caliber has emerged in the last 50 years! And," he added, "besides his genius, one can note his amazing humility and fine character throughout every word he writes." Then he looked up at the man. "You come from Butzatz. Have you ever heard of a young man called Meshulam Igra?"

The community leader didn't emit a verbal response. He simply fainted.

When he came to, he recounted the entire episode that occurred many years back, that Rabbi Igra was meant to be his son-in-law, but the match was broken over coffee grounds. The rabbi looked up at him and shook his head sadly. "Is that so?" he muttered. The man nodded. Then the Rav of Hamburg looked at the man and said, "Faint again!"

Throughout its history, perhaps the greatest undoing of our nation is the non-acceptance of great leaders. Among our midst exist diamonds, but they are often treated like raw coal. There is a most popular song, sung in the yeshiva world on all holidays, "*Moshe emes v'Toraso emes.* Moshe is true, and his Torah is true." It is sung fervently — the question is do we truly believe it?

Yet the indivisibility of Torah and its teachers, the understanding of the two as inseparable in their validity, is fundamental throughout the writings of Rambam and all scholars of Torah Judaism. Without recognizing the greatness of our leaders, we would be lost. Therefore, Hashem did not want the rebellion against Moshe to subside with just one action. He took three very different miracles — splitting the earth, a consuming fire, and budding the dry staff — to reiterate a most important point that still sustains us today. If we do not realize from where our strength comes, Hashem will remind us. And if we, Heaven forbid, forget, He will tell us to faint again!

Parshas Chukas

Snake Eyes

This *parsha* is hardly one of Moshe's easiest ones. Throughout the entire portion, Moshe suffered a series of disappointments and tragedies. First, his sister Miriam died. Then the miraculous well ceased to flow from the rock that traveled with the Jewish nation. When the people complained bitterly, Moshe was told to talk to the rock, and it would produce water. But Moshe did not talk to the rock; instead, he hit it. For that, he was censured by Hashem for distorting His command. As a punishment, Moshe did not enter *Eretz Yisrael*. Indeed, he and Ahron both died in the desert.

The setbacks did not end there, either. Moshe sent messengers to the king of Edom, imploring him to allow the Children of Israel, cousins of the Edomites, to journey through their land. "We will," the Jews promised, "purchase supplies from the citizens of Edom and only take the main roads" (*Numbers 20:14-19*). Yet Edom responded with an emphatic no and threatened war. Moshe acquiesced and took the long route toward the land of Israel.

As if all this is not enough, the Torah tells us of another blow to Moshe — the death of his only brother Ahron. Moshe was left alone, with neither Miriam nor Ahron to support him. What's more, the death of Ahron brought no tranquility, for immediately after it the Jews were attacked by the King of Arad in the south. (The Talmud tells us that he was our evil nemesis Amalek). Although the Jews won the battle, the Torah tells us that they were still not satisfied. Indeed, they verbally attacked Moshe and Hashem, complaining, "Why did you bring us to die in this wilderness with no food or water, and our souls are disgusted with the light fare of manna!" *(Numbers 21:5)*

Hashem was hardly quiescent. Fiery snakes attacked the people, but Moshe, despite the trials and tribulation he had endured, had only one thing on his mind. While many people would have given up, Moshe had strength, courage, and love of *B'nai Yisrael* to plead on behalf of his nation to Hashem: "Stop the snakes!"

As an answer, Hashem told Moshe to make a copper snake and put it on a stick; people who were bitten had to gaze at the snake to be cured. And it was so: Moshe made the snake, and the afflicted were healed. The *Mishnah* in *Rosh Hashana* asks rhetorically, does a snake actually cure? Of course not! The *Mishnah* goes on to explain that it was not the snake which healed, but rather the snake was merely a symbol for the nation to think about heaven and repent.

The obvious mystery strikes every reader of the Torah. Why would the snake be an impetus to *teshuva*? (Just as, parenthetically, a snake twisted round a staff has become the symbol of those who are divinely guided to heal the very wounds that it inflicts). Why didn't Moshe put a sacred scroll on the stick? Why did the symbol of fiery venom and certain death motivate the nation to repent? What transformed the very item we loathe and fear into the symbol of our cure?

It was two decades before the Declaration of Independence. The Redcoats were tired of the Colonists and had made sure the Americans knew it. Indeed, the British sang a song — and while historians are not sure if the tune was of French, Spanish, or German origin, its lyrics were English and meant to taunt. The silly song mocked the Colonists, and the British sang it outside the patriots' meeting places — even in front of their houses of worship. While the song was intended to scare the Americans into submission, it did not.

In fact, a strange thing happened to the very tune used to demoralize the fledgling nation: the Americans stole it, and the ragtag brigades used it against their enemy. They sang it in battle. They sang it in victory. They even sang it in defeat! Finally, it was played and sung by the victorious Colonial Army

at the surrender of Lord Cornwallis at Yorktown in 1781.

The song that was meant to mock had become a ballad of honor and was incorporated into the melodies and compositions that glorified the victories of the Colonial Army. It was even highlighted in Benjamin Carr's *Federal Overture* written in 1794!

So the very words that were meant to taunt and irritate were used to celebrate, and the tune that was meant to jeer became the nation's cheer. Even today every American child knows it and sings it proudly: "Yankee Doodle!"

How did Moshe survive the ordeals, suffering, and hardship that plagued him through most of his career? In his earliest meeting with Hashem, Moshe endured a very frightening experience: Hashem told him to throw down his staff — and then transformed it into a vicious snake. When Moshe ran, Hashem told Moshe to confront the snake and grab it. When he did, the snake miraculously turned back into a very benign stick (*Exodus 4:1-5*). As such, Moshe taught that very lesson to *Klal Yisrael*: snake venom is actually the antidote to the bite!

It is easy to run from your fears and horrors, and sometimes you may be running from the very monster that bit you. But if you confront the monster with fire in your eyes and sincerity in your heart, then you have nothing to fear. The very obstacles that caused our trepidations, the challenges and antagonistic experiences that caused us to falter, can be the impetus for our growth. Because with the right frame of mind, the very animal that took control of you is not only harmless, it becomes your source of strength.

Parshas Balak

Sorry for Nothing

We are all fascinated by inanimate objects or animals that speak. Indeed, the '60s had TV viewers *kvelling* over talking horses, even talking cars. And today a multi-billion-dollar industry thrives on the concept of a talking mouse! But in this portion a talking animal is no joke, as the Torah tells us about a talking animal that brought no laughs to its rider — and teaches a serious lesson to us all.

Bilaam, the greatest prophet that the gentile world had seen, was hired by Balak, King of Moab, for one mission: to curse the Jews. Bilaam's initial feigned reluctance was quickly changed to exuberance when offers of honors and great wealth were added as a signing bonus. First thing in the morning, he saddled his trusted donkey and was on his way. Bilaam's plan was to travel to an overlook, where he could cast his spell on the Jewish nation as it camped innocently below.

But Hashem had different plans. As Bilaam's donkey ambled toward a narrow passage, it saw a frightening sight: an angel, with a sword thrust forward, blocked its path. The beast turned off the road into a field, and Bilaam struck the animal to get it back on the road. But again the angel stood in the passageway, and the poor donkey, in fear, squeezed tightly against a wall, pressing Bilaam's leg against the stones. The great prophet, who so haughtily straddled the donkey, did not see the angelic figure and reacted violently. Again he hit his donkey, this time harder. But the angel did not retreat; instead, he approached the donkey and its rider. Suddenly, the donkey crouched in panic, and Bilaam struck it again. But that time, the donkey did not act like a mule; instead, it spoke up. Miraculously, Hashem gave it the power of speech, and it asked Bilaam, "Why did you hit me? Aren't I the same animal that you have ridden your entire life? Should not my strange behavior give cause for concern?" (*Numbers 22:28*)

When the angel, sword in hand, finally revealed himself, and chided Bilaam for striking the innocent animal, Bilaam was left speechless save for one sentence. "I have sinned, for I did not know that you were standing opposite me on the road. And if you want, I shall return" (*Numbers 22:34*).

Why did Bilaam immediately admit sin? If he could not see the angel, why did he admit guilt? Further, many riders would hit a donkey that presses their feet against the wall or crouches down amidst a group of a king's officers. Bilaam should have simply stated, "I did not know you were there and thought my beast was acting in a manner that required discipline." So why the apology?

On one of the final days of the Six Day War, Israeli troops breached enemy fortifications and fought their way through the ancient passageways of Jerusalem. As if Divine gravitational force was pulling them, one group of soldiers dodged the Jordanian bullets and proceeded until there was no reason to continue: they had reached the *Kotel Hamaravi*, the Western Wall, the holiest place in Judaism, the site of both the First and Second Temples. The young men, some of whom had had a yeshiva education, stood in awe and began to cry in unison, "The *Kotel* had been liberated!"

One young soldier, who grew up on a completely secular kibbutz in the northern portion of the state, gazed at the sight of his comrades crying like children as they stared up at the ancient stones. Suddenly, he, too began to wail.

One of the religious soldiers, who had engaged in countless debates with him, put his arm around him and asked, "I don't understand. To us, the *Kotel* means so much. It is our link with the Temple and the holy service. We have just liberated the holiest place in our heritage. This is the most moving experience of our lives. But you, " he paused, "you have always stated

that this does not mean anything to you. So, why are you crying?"

The young soldier looked at his friend, and amidst his tears simply stated, "I am crying because I am not crying."

Bilaam, the greatest of gentile prophets, realized that something had to be wrong. A simple donkey saw the revelation of an angel, but Bilaam did not. He understood that there are experiences he should have been able to grasp and appreciate — and if he didn't, it was not his donkey's fault. And it was not an angel's fault, it was *his* fault. Bilaam realized then and there that it was he who was lacking.

How often does God cry out to us in newspaper headlines — earthquakes, wildfires, or human tragedies? Like Bilaam, we should stare at the sight and see a Divine figure standing with an outstretched sword. But we do not. We flip the paper, and we strike the donkeys. Instead, we should cry at the tragedies of life — and if we do not realize what they are, then we should cry about that. For then one day we will all smile. Forever.

Parshas Pinchas

Shmaltz Droppings

A very humbling experience occurred to Moshe in this portion, as the Torah tells how the five daughters of Zelafchad approached him with a serious question. Previously, the Torah had only taught the laws of inheritance for male descendants. "Our father, Zelafchad, had no sons," they explained, "and he died in the desert, leaving us, his daughters. Can we, too, inherit, and take a share in the land of Israel?" (*Numbers 27:3-5*)

Wholly out of character, Moshe did not have an answer – and brought the question to God Himself. Rashi explains the reason that Moshe was at a loss: he was punished for something he had said many years prior. His father-in-law, Yisro, had suggested that Moshe create a system of judges on different levels. Depending on the severity of a case, there would be the proper judges to hear it. Simple cases would go to lower-level judges, while more difficult cases would go to superior adjudicators.

It was an excellent system, but Moshe made one statement of which Hashem did not approve. Moshe told the judges, "The small matters you shall judge, and the difficult ones bring to me" (*Deuteronomy 1:17*). In this *parsha,* Hashem showed Moshe that he, too, could forget a law.

When Moshe forgot the law of a daughter's inheritance, he was forced to present the case to Hashem. But what did Moshe actually do wrong? After all, he was the acknowledged leader and teacher of the Jewish people. He had taught them all they knew; to whom else should they have brought difficult cases — if not to him? Why was it improper for Moshe to tell them that he was the final authority for any difficult matter?

The author of the *Chamudos Daniel*, the *Rav* of Horodna, lived in dire poverty, with wages so low there was barely enough to feed his family more than black bread and kasha. One evening, he was surprised to see a bit of *shmaltz* mixed in the groats and inquired of his wife about the fatty additive to the otherwise dry fare.

"Our neighbor was making chicken today and gave me a bit of the fat. I decided to add it to the kasha," his wife replied proudly.

Reb Daniel immediately finished his food, recited the grace after meals, and excused himself from the table. He immediately summoned a few community leaders for a meeting. "My wife unknowingly took a bribe today," he declared. "She received a gift from the wife of a man who is due to see me in *Bais Din* on an issue. I request to exclude myself immediately from the case, as I am no longer worthy to sit in judgment on it!"

Commentaries explain Moshe's directive to the judges in an interesting light. Difficult did not mean *legally* complex – it meant *morally* complex. For there are indeed difficult and complex legal issues. And there are issues that concern large amounts of money. For those, Moshe had full faith in his judges. But Moshe was wary of the difficult moral issues involved in many cases. Widows and orphans against steel magnates; relatives or friends who stand in judicial review — those are the difficult issues that Moshe insisted to hear. And while Moshe seemed to imply that he is above such issues, here he found himself in a moral bind.

The Chofetz Chaim explains that the moment that Moshe heard the daughters of Zelafchad say, "our father was not involved in Korach's uprising," they added a bit of *shmaltz* to the picture. And when they ended with the request to be included in the inheritance, Moshe felt that his judgment was tainted. He understood that only Hashem Himself could render an objective opinion.

In our lives, we constantly make decisions — and we assume them to be fair, unbiased, and accurate. But often we forget that we are subtly savoring *shmaltz* droppings that may bias our bland opinions. And unless we think hard and dry, we may never taste the difference.

Parshas Matos

Oath of Office

The portion of *Matos* begins with the laws governing commitments and pledges. In Torah law, words are not taken lightly, and when one makes an oath, the implications are exacting. The portion begins, "Moshe spoke to the *Roshei Hamatos* (the heads of the tribes), saying: This is the thing that Hashem commanded. If a man takes a vow to Hashem, or swears to enact a prohibition upon himself, he shall not desecrate his word; whatever he said he shall do" (*Numbers 30:2-3*). The portion continues to discuss vows that one places upon himself, as well as vows that are between husbands and wives and fathers and daughters. The Torah then details the complex laws of both the obligations and revocation of vows.

What is strikingly different in this portion is the way it was transmitted. Normally, the Torah does not talk about teaching the law to the heads of the tribes. In *Parshas Ki Sisa*, for example, the Torah states that Moshe first taught Ahron, Ahron's children, the tribal elders, and only then all of Israel (*Exodus 34:31-32*).

The Torah hardly ever reiterates that point. Yet here, in *Matos*, Moshe emphasized his directive to the heads of the tribes. Why? Wasn't the whole Torah given to them first? Why repeat that fact here?

Rashi explains that Moshe gave honor to the elders and leaders because they play such a vital role in the laws of vows. Unlike other judicial actions, the power of annulment of vows is accomplished by experts who can rule on vows and have the ability to decide which are valid and which are inconsequential. In addition, experts can evaluate vows that may have been made under duress or out of fear and render them void. Therefore, unlike his restatement of other commandments, Moshe specified the role of the leaders in reference to vows.

But perhaps there is another significance to specifying the role of elders when talking about vows.

Rabbi Akiva Eiger was a world-renowned Talmudic sage who wrote on almost every aspect of the Torah. However, as the Rabbi of Pozen, which was part of the Austrio-Hungarian Empire, his custom was to defer responding to questions that were sent from outside his country. After all, he felt that the stature of other rabbis would be diminished if all their congregants sent their questions to an out-of-town rabbi — even one with his credentials and stature.

Nevertheless, he once received a letter from Bialostock, Poland, to which he did respond.

Rabbi Akiva Eiger began his response, "Although I am unworthy of answering questions from distant lands that are filled with great rabbis and *halachic* scholars, and surely Poland is not lacking in either, this time I will answer." Then he added his reason.

"A few months back," he wrote, "I was at a *simcha* at which someone from your town said that he would write me concerning a difficult matter. Though I did not encourage him to do so, I also did not discourage him. In fact, I may have even nodded my head slightly. That may have been taken as a commitment to answer the question. And if I even appeared to have consented, I surely do not want to appear as if I have reneged on a commitment."

The Torah transmits the laws of oaths through the heads of each tribe because it wants to reiterate to them the importance of a leader's adherence to commitment. The eyes of a nation are focused on their words and their promises. It is therefore only fitting that those, who bear the great responsibility of assuring their tribes of their needs and requests, should be the very ones who transmit those laws.

Now, unfortunately, the words of contemporary leaders and elected officials don't mean much. As an Israeli diplomat once said, "It is our experience that political leaders do not always mean the opposite of what they say."

The Torah speaks differently, however, for it hands the responsibility of the burden of language upon those who are faced with the greatest challenge to keep their word. The actions of Torah leaders should cause others to resonate, "It is our experience that political leaders never mean the opposite of what they say."

Torah leaders must personify the commitment to the idea that "all that will come out of his mouth he shall keep." Indeed, it is no wonder that the Torah specifies the role of the tribal leaders. For when the leaders keep their word, the nation keeps its vision.

Parshas Masei

Dead First

Parshas Masei discusses the sojourns of *Klal Yisrael* through the desert. It focuses on the many stops that the Jewish nation made, hinting at the ensuing incidents that occurred with each stop.

But one verse seems to divert attention from the Jews' travels and chooses to focus on a scene occurring miles away. The Torah tells us that "[the Jews] journeyed from Ramses on the fifteenth day of the first month and went forth with a *yad ramah* (upraised hand) to the eyes of all Egyptians" (*Numbers* 33:3). The Torah then inserts a seemingly irrelevant detail, one that seems to be insignificant if not anticlimactic to the great tragedy that befell the Egyptians and the miraculous Exodus of the Jews. It reverts to a scene that takes place back in Egypt in the days following the Jews' departure from Egypt. "The Egyptians were burying their dead, whom Hashem had struck, every firstborn, and in their gods Hashem meted justice" (*ibid*,v.4).

Isn't this a mere historical detail? Why even mention it? In fact, if it were to mention anything, the Torah should have written "and the Egyptians were mourning their firstborn-dead whom Hashem miraculously smote on the prior night."

It seems that the Torah placed this *posuk* specifically here as a significant lesson — one of the lessons of the Exodus.

In the famous work, *A Tzaddik in our Times,* Simcha Raz relates an amazing story about Rabbi Aryeh Levin, the *tzaddik* of Jerusalem: It was mid-May 1948, bombs were raining on central Jerusalem, no street was safe and no home a haven. Yet it was

during a bomb attack that Samuel Weingarten, a bank cashier who volunteered for civil defense, spotted the holy sage Rabbi Aryeh Levin, maneuvering his way, dodging craters below and bombs from above, in a desperate effort to get somewhere. His steps were careful and calculated and he strode with confidence, a clear destination in mind.

"Rabbi!" Weingarten shouted above the din. "Where are you going? A Jew must guard his soul! They are shooting at us! Get inside a shelter!"

Rabbi Levin was not fazed. "I am on my way to do the greatest *mitzvah.* There are forty deceased souls in the Bikur Cholim Hospital, with no one to guard them. The only watchmen are the human jackals who cut their fingers to remove their jewelry. I am rounding up volunteers to guard them. The bombs will have to find different addresses."

In addition to exacting every detail of how a Jew should live his life, the Torah is also a guidebook to an entire world on what is ethically correct. The foundations set forth in the Torah, its myriad principles, form the core of ethical behavior even for the basest of people. Murder, incest, and other abominable acts are deplored in the Torah. Some are denoted with the words *toaivah,* abomination, others with disgust and some with depictions of Heavenly retribution, be it the Flood or the destruction of S'dom. Those stories are lessons for civilization. They are standards required for every inhabitant of planet Earth. These aspects of the Torah serve as a moral compass. They come together with the ethos of kindness and compassion that can be surely garnered by those who are students of the Torah.

So if we take a step back in time and understand what was going on in the minds of the Egyptians, and what the Torah deems important to mention, perhaps we can preserve another moral lesson that may better inspire our generation with proper values.

Imagine! For 210 years the Jews were captive in Egypt. Despite miraculous plagues, never heard of or seen before in the history of civilization, the Egyptians held on. They were not letting go! Not a threat of disaster, nor its execution, shook their resolve or diminished the Egyptians' desire to maintain their hold on the Jews. Not blood, boils, locusts, or any other plague, daunted them. Even when the Jews finally left, the Egyptians chased after them. But not immediately. The Torah tells us that something else was more important. Something was even worth giving the Jews an enormous head-start. Something was worth losing the very nation that their firstborn died to keep. It was all for the sake of one solemn principle — the honor and burial of the dead.

And so the Torah tells us that despite the political ramifications that occurred with the Exodus, something else was on Egypt's mind. Maybe the actions of that primitive nation should give the world a perspective about what really matters. If an ancient nation was willing to give up its century-old national pride, the loss of the largest single work-force in history for the honor of the dead, shouldn't every nation give thought to their priorities as well? Shouldn't they maintain the honor of those buried instead of covering them with a shopping mall, or uprooting them for a new roadway, or even removing them to be inspected and gawked at in a museum? We may not learn many great moral lessons from the Egyptians, but this one is certainly worthwhile.

Even if in the war of wits you come in dead last, in the war of morality make sure you come in dead first.

ספר דברים

The Book of Deuteronomy

Parshas Devorim

Family Feuds

Though blood, it is said, is thicker than water, it is hardly the sole criterion to hold back the sword. After all, Yaakov's brother Esav is the father of Edom and grandfather of Amalek — and there is no love lost between Israel and these two nations.

Yet the Torah tells us about two families — cousins, albeit very distant — against whom we may not wage war. Moshe told the Children of Israel that Hashem told him, "you may not provoke war with Moav... for to the children of Lot I have given Ar as an inheritance" (*Deuteronomy 2:9*). The Moavites were descendants of Lot, Avraham's nephew. Their forebear, Moav, was fathered through an incestuous union of Lot and his eldest daughter — who named him, unabashedly, *Mo Av,* "from my father."

Rashi points out that even though the Jews were forbidden to wage war with Moav, they were permitted to antagonize, intimidate, and even provoke them. That is why Moav's King Balak engaged the evil prophet Bilaam to curse the Jews: Moav was afraid of them.

The descendants of Ammon, on the other hand, fared better. Though Ammon, descended from another incestuous relationship between Lot and his younger daughter, the name *Ben-Ami,* "the son of my nation," hides that shameful act. Therefore, in the merit of the Ammonites' mother's modesty, the Jews were not permitted to antagonize her descendants, the nation of Ammon.

Indeed, Lot's children were treated better than any other folk, including closer relatives. For example, there is no warning not to taunt or attack the children of Ishmael, Avraham's own son. Why doesn't their relationship prevent this, as it seems to with Lot? The *Midrash* explains that it is not Lot's blood relationship to Avraham that sheathed our swords, instead it is our gratitude.

How is that?

Twenty-five years prior to the destruction of S'dom, Lot, in a small way, saved Avraham's life. When Avraham and Sora went to Egypt, they knew the custom was to kill the husbands of beautiful wives and send them to Pharoah's harem. Fearing certain death, Avraham therefore claimed that Sora was his sister. Lot, who was with Avraham and Sora and could have divulged the truth, did not. Therefore, because Lot went along with the ploy, and did not give up Avraham and Sora, his children were rewarded: the Jews could never wage war on them.

Yet that merit does not stand on its own. It seems that Lot's discretion at the Egyptian border was enough to stop the Jews from waging all-out war against his descendants. However, instilling fear was not ruled out. Why?

When Napoleon was fleeing the Russian Army after his defeat in 1812, he escaped into the home of a peasant. "Please hide me," he cried. "When I return to my throne in Paris, I will reward you greatly!"

The farmer hid the Emperor under a bed, covering him with some old rags. Moments later, Russian soldiers burst into the tiny home looking for their prey. The Russians ransacked the cottage and prodded the bed with sticks and swords — yet Napoleon was unharmed. When they left, Napoleon crawled out from under his hiding place and reiterated his pledge. "When I get to Paris, I will call for you. I promise you anything you wish!"

Months later, the farmer was summoned to the palace, where he was allowed an audience with Napoleon. After conferring gold and silver upon the pauper, the Emperor asked the question: "Ask me anything you want, and I will respond in kind."

The man just looked down at his feet and smiled. "Oh, Emperor, I really don't want much. Just one small thing."

Napoleon's eyes widened. "And what is that?"

The farmer gathered his courage. "How did you feel when they were poking their swords through the bed?"

Napoleon flew into a rage. "Is this what you came to request? Is this the way you treat the Emperor of France? Arrest this man," he shouted to the guards. "I want him shot."

The man turned white as they led him to the wall of the outer courtyard. Napoleon accompanied them and declared that he would count to three and the firing squad would do its duty.

The man was bound, gagged, blindfolded, and placed in front of the firing squad.

"One!" shouted the Emperor. The soldiers aimed their rifles. "Two," screamed the Emperor. The soldiers cocked their triggers.

Suddenly, Napoleon held up his hand. He motioned to the soldiers to lower their arms. He walked over to the innocent man waiting to be executed and removed the blindfold. Then he put his arm around the man's shoulder and whispered in his ear, "That is how I felt!"

Lot's descendants were spared war with the Jews because Lot did not hand Avraham over to be killed. But he never alleviated Avraham's fears while traveling to Egypt — fears that pierced the heart of Avraham during the entire journey. Kindness must be done with graciousness. If Lot was supportive of Avraham, he should have been a true, unwavering comrade. And his merit should have been for great loyalty and not for his last-second decision not to hand Avraham over to Egyptian authorities. While Lot may have saved Avraham from certain death, he did not spare him the fear of it. So his descendants, the Moavites, albeit released from war, are reminded that though it may be meritorious to spare one from the spear, it is even better to spare one from its fear!

Parshas Voeschanan

Your Money or Your Life

A most difficult piece of Talmud is based on a verse from this portion, one that thousands of Jews read twice daily — some even more. It's a verse from the *Shema.*

The second verse of the paragraph reads, "You shall love Hashem, your God, with all your heart, all your soul, and all your wealth" (*Deuteronomy 6:5*). The Talmud in Tractate *Berachos* is concerned: "Why is it necessary to state, 'with all your soul and with all your money?' Does not simple reasoning dictate that if one must give his soul for God, then surely he must also give his money?"

The Talmud answers that "If someone values his life more than his money, for him the Torah writes, 'love Hashem with all your soul.' And for someone who values his money over his life, for him the Torah says, 'with all your money.' "

The question is obvious: how could anyone hesitate when asked the question "your money or your life?"

In fact, one of the classic scenes of 1950s American humor depicts this strange farce, in which money may be valued over one's existence.

Jack Benny, a comedian whose character was known for his penny-pinching and stingy antics, portrayed just that charade. When accosted by a masked bandit who confronted him with the menacing statement, "Your money or your life!" Mr. Benny hesitated. After a long silence the nervous hold-up man prodded him, "Well? Your money or your life!"

Mr. Benny snapped back defiantly, "I'm thinking!"

Taken purely as comedy, we all chuckle. However, as a point of Jewish ethos on which theological values are based, why does the Torah couch its instructions with an ethical anomaly? Why does the Torah spend extra words to include in its entreaty those who value wealth over health? Finally, doesn't the fact that the Talmud singles them out with a very spiritual directive, "for those to whom wealth is more important than life, love G-d with all your money," lend credence to a doctrine that is the antithesis of Torah?

While Rabbi Mendel Kaplan, of blessed memory, was a teacher in Chicago, he knew a man who collected newspapers. Indeed, the man had gathered so many periodicals that he was about to be thrown out of his apartment. Concerned, Rabbi Kaplan rented a storage garage and a U-Haul® for the man's papers, and so the otherwise normal person had a repository for his idiosyncrasy. When chided by others for spending so much time and expense on such a quirk, Reb Mendel explained, "His newspapers are as important to him as our furniture is to us. How can you make light of his feelings?"

We all might like to see a Torah based only on the *practical* applications of lofty superhuman criteria. Yet the Torah is honest — and practical — regarding the true nature of its mortal adherents. Not only does Torah convey idealism and relate it to spirituality, the Torah also takes a strong hold of the practical fallacies of the human psyche and tries to channel those feelings, however misguided, to uplift the human soul.

Over the desk of many major executives, on display for all employees to see, hangs the sign, "Time is Money."

Yet even though time is life, that is not a motivator! The only way the sign motivates workers is when it equates time with money.

There are people who go bungee-jumping and skydiving, yet keep their money under their mattresses because banks are too risky! And so the Torah talks to those people as well!

When the *Shema* offers a simile to define the great love one should have for his Creator, it does not stop at the lofty concept of love for life. The *Shema* speaks also to the base instincts of materialism as well. "If you can't manifest love with love of life, then let's talk practically as well. Manifest your love with love of money. Love Hashem even more than money!" It may not be divine, but it works. Because even though we all have our principles, we all have our quirks and priorities. Like Reb Mendel's old friend, we all have our newspapers as well.

Parshas Ekev

Perpetual Care

Some things get special attention, and the land of Israel is one of them. The Torah tells us in this portion that *Eretz Israel* is a land "that Hashem constantly watches, from the beginning of the year until the end of the year" (*Deuteronomy 11:12*).

It is an amazing verse, one that declares "the eyes" of a very personal God to be supervising a seemingly inanimate object, His most beloved piece of real estate, with constant concern. And though the commentaries discuss the special significance of this particular surveillance, as opposed to everything in the world that is under Hashem's ever-present vigilance, there arises a question. If everything is always under guard, what makes Israel so special?

In the early 1980s, my grandfather, Rabbi Yaakov Kamenetzky, of blessed memory, suffered an angina attack, and his doctor strongly recommended that he undergo an angiogram, a difficult and sometimes dangerous procedure for a man of advanced age. At the time, my younger brother, Reb Zvi, was a student at the Ponovez Yeshiva in B'nai Brak. In addition to his own prayers on behalf of our grandfather, he immediately resolved to approach his *Rosh Yeshiva,* HaGaon Rabbi Eliezer Menachem Shach, *shlit"a,* with a request to pray for Reb Yaakov's welfare.

According to Jewish tradition, when you pray for the welfare of an individual, you identify the party by mentioning him or her together with his or her mother's name. Thus Moshe's name would be

Moshe ben Yocheved (Moshe the son of Yocheved). And so on.

My brother knew that he had to present Rav Shach with our grandfather's name, Yaakov, and the name of Reb Yaakov's mother. But that was no easy feat, since Zvi did not know her name. Moreover, at the time of the angina attack, Reb Yaakov was over 90 years old and in excellent health. Indeed, Zvi could not recall a time when he had mentioned our grandfather's name in the *Mi Shebairach* prayers for the sick. Since Zvi was too embarrassed to approach Rav Shach without Reb Yaakov's mother's name, he searched throughout B'nai Brak, attempting to find someone who might know the name of Reb Yaakov's mother.

Visiting the homes of second cousins and other relatives, my brother inquired widely, but no one knew. Finally, he went to a nephew of Reb Yaakov, who lived in B'nai Brak, who told my brother that Reb Yaakov's mother was named Etka.

Armed with the information and an update on my grandfather's condition, he approached the home of Rav Shach.

The elderly sage invited my brother into his sparsely furnished dining room and asked him to take a seat. The elderly Rosh Yeshiva then sat next to a wooden table standing directly under a large bulb illuminating the tomes that lay open in front of him. The *Rosh Yeshiva* looked up from the Talmudic passage he had been contemplating and smiled at my brother. The great sage knew my brother and his lineage and asked how he was feeling. Then he inquired about Reb Yaakov.

My brother turned white. "That is exactly why I came," he stammered. Immediately, Rav Shach's face filled with consternation. My brother continued, "You see, my grandfather is not feeling well and must undergo a procedure. I came to inform the..."

Rav Shach jumped up from his chair and exclaimed, "We must say a special prayer for Reb Yaakov ben Etka!"

My brother stood opened-mouthed and could not contain himself. "Rebbe," he began meekly, "for the last 12 hours I have been trying to find out my great-grandmother's name in order to present it to the Rosh Yeshiva. Now I see that the Rosh Yeshiva knows the name already. How is that?"

Rav Shach explained. "Years ago, your grandfather visited *Eretz Yisrael.* After meeting him, I asked him for his mother's name. You see, I could not imagine a Jewish world without a healthy Reb Yaakov, so there is not a single day that goes by that I do not say a special prayer for his welfare!"

There is a lesson that Hashem tells us with these words. Sometimes we think that the Jewish Land is on autopilot, but Hashem tells us that it is not. His eyes are on it 365 days a year, 24 hours a day. And though we all care for and love *Eretz Yisrael,* perhaps we, too, should mimic that attitude. We, too, should not be able to imagine a world without a stable and healthy Israel. And, like Hashem, we should also have it constantly in our hearts and minds — not only during a crisis when the storm clouds are brewing, but from "the beginning of the year until the end," even when the sun is shining down on it.

PARSHAS RE'EH

Brotherly Give

Charity, one of the foundations of Jewish life, begins at home. The Torah tells us various times in this portion to give generously and with an open heart. Nevertheless, while enjoining us to give, the Torah also seems to qualify the recipient.

"If there shall be a destitute person among you from any of your brethren in any of your cities ... you shall not harden your heart or close your hand against your destitute brother." Indeed, Hashem exhorts the nation to "open your hand to him." Then the Torah tells us that "destitute people will not cease to exist, therefore I command you, saying, 'You shall surely open your hand to your brother, your poor, and your destitute in your land'" (*Deuteronomy 15:7-12*).

What is noteworthy is the constant use of the phrase "your brother, your poor." Why would one not give to his own brother, and is there a difference if the poor person is a brother or a stranger?

Is it not sufficient to say "give to your brother?" Is it not enough to say "give to your poor?"

Russia's Tsar Alexander I triumphantly visited France after the defeat of Napoleon in the early part of the 1800s. To show his good will, he attended a fund-raising event at one of the local hospitals, where women went around with plates accepting contributions. That night, a beautiful young girl was given the task of asking the Tsar for a contribution.

Cautiously, she approached the mighty emperor, curtsied, and presented the collection plate. The Tsar

looked at her and smiled. Then he dropped two gold coins on the plate, adding, "This is for your beautiful, bright eyes."

The young maiden did not move. Instead, she curtsied one more time, gently nudging the plate forward once again.

The Tsar looked puzzled. "I have just given you," he barked. "You want more?"

"Yes, sire," she replied. "Now I want something for the poor people."

The Torah's descriptive words, "your brother, your poor," are more than a qualifying narrative. They do more than specify the type of pauper we should give to. Instead, the words are telling us about a distinct philosophy of charitable giving.

Often, I raise money for our yeshiva, or for other causes, and I am told, "Rabbi, I really don't know anything about your yeshiva, and I really don't know much about that particular person in need, but I like *you,* so here's a contribution."

Of course, charity in any form is wonderful, but the Torah tells us here, "give to your brother, your poor."

One must consider both factors, each on its own merit.

Even if he is not "your brother," even if the institution or individual is not close, find out about the particular need of the individual or cause, and give because there is a need — give to your poor.

The Torah knows that we often give charity because one is our brother: it knows that we give for beautiful bright eyes. Here, the Torah tells us to give for another cause. It tells us to give for an additional reason other than that he is our brother, our kin. We must give to him because of his poverty as well.

Parshas Shoftim

It's Just Justice

The pursuit of justice is a tenet of any civilized society, and the Torah defines that principle in a clear and unambiguous way. *"Tzedek, tzedek tirdof* — righteousness, righteousness you shall pursue" (*Deuteronomy 16:20*).

The Torah tells us not only to *seek* righteousness but also to *pursue* it. Yet, while the Torah seems to tell us to chase justice with vigilance and fervor, the words of the verse amplify the pursuit of righteousness more than righteousness itself.

What's more, the Torah repeats the word righteousness but not the word pursue. Would it not have been more appropriate to stress the word pursue rather than the word righteousness?

Second, what does "righteousness, righteousness" mean? Isn't one righteousness enough? What is double righteousness?

Finally, shouldn't we double our efforts in its pursuit? Shouldn't the Torah have said, "Pursue, oh, pursue righteousness" instead of telling us, "Righteousness, righteousness you shall pursue?" Isn't the pursuit of righteousness the main goal? Doesn't the Torah want to stress the passionate pursuit of righteousness? Obviously, the double expression, "righteousness, righteousness" contains a poignant message — but what is it?

Veteran news reporter David Brinkley surveyed the Washington scene back in September, 1992, and reported a very interesting event.

Washington, DC, derives a great portion of revenue from traffic tickets. In fact, $50 million a year is raised from tickets for moving violations, expired inspection

stickers, overdue registrations, and, of course, the inescapable plethora of expired parking meters.

A traffic officer was on a Washington curb writing a ticket for an illegally parked car. As he was writing the ticket, a thief had the audacity to come by with a screwdriver and steal the car's license plate.

The officer did not stop him. He just waited until the thief had finished. Then he gave the car another ticket — for parking on a public street with no license plate.

Sometimes justice is overwhelmed by the pursuit of it. The Torah tells us what type of righteousness to pursue — not just plain righteousness, but rather "righteous righteousness." There is just justice, and there is a system of laws that often goes out of control. Therefore, the Torah exhorts us not only to seek justice but also to pursue a just justice.

It is said that during the 1930s, when the saintly Rabbi Yisroel Meir haKohen of Radin, better known as the Chofetz Chaim, was in his 90s, he wanted to live the last years of his life in *Eretz Yisrael*. However, he was unable to obtain a Polish passport because the Polish government required him to produce either an official birth certificate or to bring forward two witnesses who were there at his birth! All of that was in pursuit of an unjust code of law. That's why the Torah tells us not only to be vigilant in the pursuit of righteousness, but also to be righteous in its pursuit as well!

Parshas Ki Saytzay

Dead Man Falling

Liability. Personal responsibility and the utmost care for fellow humans were discussed in the Torah long before lawyers and lawsuits appeared on the judicial scene.

The Torah warns us in this portion that "when you will build a new house, you shall make a fence for your roof so that you shall not place blood in your house if a fallen one falls from it" (*Deuteronomy 22:8*). Simply stated, the Torah warns us to ensure that our homes are not unsafe and to take precautionary measures to ensure the safety of occupants and visitors alike.

Noteworthy, however, is the difficult expression, "in your house if a fallen one falls from it." Though one who falls is obviously the fallen one, he is not "a fallen one" until he actually falls. Why, then, does the Torah state that "the fallen one falls from it?" Shouldn't it rather have said when the "standing one shall fall from it?"

The Supreme Commander of all Allied forces, General Dwight D. Eisenhower, was inspecting a position held by the British in North Africa. Accompanied by the officer in command, Ike was touring the area in his jeep when all of a sudden a German plane came sweeping down, guns blazing from its turrets. The British officer jammed on his brakes, hauled the American general from the jeep, pushed him into a ditch, and lay on top of him until the threat passed.

When the enemy was out of sight, the officer helped Eisenhower to his feet and nervously inquired about his welfare. Eisenhower, touched by the young Brit's watchfulness, thanked him profusely for taking such personal precautions for his safety.

"That's all right, General," smiled the officer, "I just didn't want anything to happen to you while you were in my sector!"

The Torah alludes to the ever-pressing question of fate and destiny versus free will. Rashi comments that one who falls and gets hurt, or worse, was a marked man. After all, if not for some Divine reason, he would not have been injured. However, that is no excuse for anyone's property to be the vehicle of misfortune. While the man who falls was obviously Divinely ordained as a fallen man, just as good fortune can befall humans through other good humans, so can misfortune befall someone through careless or callous ones.

Therefore, he who has not secured his property through negligence is responsible for another's injuries regardless of what Hashem has ordained for the victim. True, he who falls is a fallen man, but if he falls on your property the Torah considers you responsible — despite the injury's Divine pre-ordinance.

The Talmud in *Gittin* states that when the first Roman General Nero Kaiser came to Jerusalem to attack it, he approached a young Jewish boy and asked him to quote a verse he had learned in his yeshiva.

The child answered by quoting *Ezekiel,* 25:14, "I will lay My vengeance upon Edom (Rome) by the hand of My people Israel." Nero Kaiser immediately exclaimed, "The Holy One wants to destroy His Temple and then wipe His hands on me?" Nero fled and became a proselyte from whom the great Rabbi Meir was descended.

Rabbi Elchonon Wasserman, of blessed memory, was in the United States in the months prior to the outbreak of World War II. Although he could have stayed here in safety, he insisted on returning to his yeshiva in Baranowitz, Poland, to be with his students whom he had left behind. While Reb Elchonon knew that his return was fraught with the danger that would ultimately claim his life, he nevertheless refused to stay in the United States claiming that, "every bullet has its address."

True faith tells us just that, that every bullet has its address, and that Hashem is the ultimate Postmaster who coordinates the delivery. The Torah alludes to the fact that he who falls was truly a fallen man — a clear implication of the concept of Divine fate and Heavenly Providence. But in doing so, the Torah also warns us that as humans, we do not have to be an accomplice to God's plans of misfortune. He will manage that alone. We must fence our properties and guard their occupants. Because our job is to be only the vehicle and intermediaries of good fortune.

Parshas Ki Savo

The Search for Meaning

This portion discusses the entry into Israel and the responsibilities that are intrinsically tied with inheriting the land. There are countless blessings which accrue if the Jewish people follow a Torah lifestyle and, unfortunately, myriad curses if such values are abandoned.

But after the litany of blessings and curses, Moshe told the nation, "You have seen everything that Hashem did before your eyes in the land of Egypt to Pharaoh and all his servants and to all the land. Your eyes beheld the great signs and wonders, but Hashem did not give you a heart to comprehend, eyes to see, or ears to hear until this day" (*Deuteronomy 29:2-3*). While Moshe was obviously referring to the day that the Jews received the Torah's understanding of events, such a statement seems to defy logic. After all, what does one need to understand about wonders? Water turning to blood, supernatural invasions of wild animals, locusts, and fire-filled hail need no special illumination to fathom God's power. Surely the splitting of the sea is as amazing an event that one could witness in any generation!

What, then, did Moshe mean when he told the nation that Hashem did not give you "a heart to comprehend, eyes to see, or ears to hear until this day?"

Rav Noach Weinberg, dean of the Aish HaTorah institutions, tells the story of the young man who came to him in search of spiritual meaning.

The young man entered the portals of Yeshiva Aish HaTorah for a few days and then decided to

leave in order to pursue his quest across the land of Israel. After two weeks of spiritual hunting, including stops at synagogues in Meah Shearim, and visits to holy sites in Tiberias and Tzefat, the student returned to Jerusalem and headed straight back to the yeshiva.

"Rabbi Weinberg," he exclaimed, "I spent two weeks traveling the length and breadth of Israel in search of spirituality, and I want you to know that I found absolutely nothing!"

Rabbi Weinberg just nodded. "You say you traveled the entire country and did not find any spirituality?"

"Yes, sir," came the resounding reply. "None whatsoever!"

"Let me ask you," the rabbi continued, "what is your opinion about the Israeli Bafoofsticks?"

"Bafoofsticks?" the student countered. "What's a Bafoofstick?"

"That's not the point," the rabbi responded. "I just want to know how you feel about them."

"About what?"

"The Bafoofsticks"

The young man looked at the Rabbi Weinberg as if the learned man had lost his mind, and tried to be as respectful as he could under the circumstances. "Rabbi!" he exclaimed in frustration, "I'd love to tell you how the Bafoofsticks were. I'd even spend the whole day discussing Bafoofsticks with you. But frankly, I honestly have no idea what in the world is a Bafoofstick! I wouldn't even know a Bafoofstick if I saw one!"

Rabbi Weinberg smiled, for he had accomplished his objective. "Tell me," he said softly. "Do you know what spirituality is?"

Moshe explained to the nation that it is possible to be mired in miracles and still not comprehend the greatness that surrounds you. One can experience miraculous revelations, but unless he focuses his heart and mind he will continue to lead his life uninspired as before.

In fact, even blessings need to be realized. In offering God's blessings, the Torah tells us, "the blessings will be upon you, and they will reach you" (*Deuteronomy 28:2*). But if blessings are upon us, of course they reach us! Why the redundancy? Once again, the Torah teaches us that it is possible to be surrounded by blessing and not realize it. There are people who have health, wealth, and great fortune, but their lives are mired in misery. They have the blessing, but it has not reached them.

Therefore, we need more than physical, or even spiritual, blessing. We need more than the experience of miraculous events. It is not enough to see miracles or receive the best of fortune. We must bring them into our lives and into our souls. Then we will be truly blessed.

Parshas Nitzavim

Heartspeak

Teshuva. It is the word of the hour, and there is no better time for the Torah to talk about it than the week before *Rosh Hashana. Teshuva* means repentance, not only taking heart but even changing heart! And in this portion, the Torah tells us that the requirements are not as difficult as one might believe. "It is not in heaven or across the sea. Rather, it is very near to you — in your mouth and in your heart — to perform" (*Deuteronomy 30:12-14*).

The Ibn Ezra comments on the three aspects of commitment that the Torah alludes to — the mouth, the heart, and the performance. In practical terms, these are commandments that outline certain thoughts and emotions, those that entail speech, and those that require action.

On a simple level, the Torah seems to discuss a process that involves commitment before action, for it takes the heart and the mouth to make a commitment before any action is performed. Thus, the Torah tells us, "it is very near to you — in your mouth and in your heart — to perform." The sequence of events, however, seems reversed. The Torah puts the mouth before the heart. Shouldn't the Torah have written, "It is very near to you — in your heart and in your mouth— to perform?" Doesn't one have to have wholehearted feelings before making verbal pledges? Why would the Torah first tell us that it is close to your mouth and then your heart?

In the years before the establishment of the State of Israel, Rabbi Aryeh Levin, the renowned *Tzaddik* of Jerusalem, visited the inmates of the British-con-

trolled Jerusalem prison every *Shabbos*. Though most of the Jewish prisoners were not observant, they quickly donned *kippot* before the revered rabbi greeted them. Then they joined in the *Shabbos* morning prayer service that Reb Aryeh had organized, and they read along with the rabbi, as if they were observant Jews.

The entire scene agitated one particularly nasty fellow named Yaakov, who tried in every way to irritate the gentle rabbi. Each *Shabbos*, for example, Yaakov purposely lit a cigarette in Reb Aryeh's face to try to disturb him. Reb Aryeh was never fazed.

One *Shabbos*, Yaakov stormed into the makeshift synagogue and snapped at the aged Rabbi.

"Why do you waste your time with these liars and fakes?" Yaakov demanded. "They are no more observant than I am. They only put the *kippot* on their heads when you come here. Furthermore, they only pray and open their mouths to God when you are here. Otherwise, they have no feeling in their hearts!"

Reb Aryeh turned to Yaakov and rebuked him with a firm but gentle voice. "Why do you slander these souls?" he asked. "They come to pray every single week. I do not look at their heads but rather in their hearts. And when I hear the prayers coming from their lips, I know that their hearts are following as well."

It was not long before Yaakov became a steady member of the prayer group.

The Torah may be hinting at a powerful message, that even though our hearts have not as yet arrived, it is still important to use our lips to communicate the commitments and speak the prayers of the Jewish People. As such, the Torah is not far away: rather, it is close and easy for your mouth. The books are available. The *siddur* is comprehensible and translated. It is very near to your lips. All you have to do is talk the talk — sincerely. Soon enough, you will walk the walk with the same sincerity as well.

Parshas Vayelech

Boundless Energy

This portion begins with the words, "And Moshe went. And he spoke to the Children of Israel saying." The Torah tells us that he went and spoke. It does not tell us where he went. Instead, it just tells us, "Moshe went." It does tell us, however, what he said. "I am 120 years old, and I can no longer come and go, as Hashem told me that I may not cross the Jordan" (*Deuteronomy 31:1-2*).

This is more than a little perplexing. If Moshe wasn't going anywhere, if he, in fact, was telling the people that he could no longer come and go, then why open the portion with the words "and Moshe went"? If not contradictory, these words certainly seem superfluous!

Indeed, if I were to write the narrative, I would have begun Moshe's final song with the words, "And Moshe told the nation, 'I am 120 years old, and I can no longer come and go, as Hashem told me that I may not cross the Jordan."

Even more paradoxical, the name of the portion is *Vayelech,* and he went. The portion that describes Moshe's final day is entitled, "and he went. " Where did he go?

The yeshiva world has semesters, and each one is called a *zman.* Winter *zman* begins on *Rosh Chodesh Cheshvan* and ends *Rosh Chodesh Nissan,* and summer *zman* begins on *Rosh Chodesh Iyar* and ends on *Tisha B'Av.*

Breaks are referred to as *bain hazmanim,* or between the semesters. Though never called a vacation, because Torah study has no vacation, the break

period is analogous to baseball's off-season: it is a time to rest up from the previous *zman* and prepare for the upcoming one.

When I studied in the Ponovez Yeshiva in B'nai Brak, a friend of mine was getting married in England the day after *Rosh Chodesh Nissan.* I figured that on my way home to America, I would stop in England and attend the wedding. I also planned to spend a few days touring the historic sights.

I approached the *Rosh Yeshiva,* Rav Dovid Povarski, of blessed memory, for permission to leave a few days before the *zman* ended. That way, I would be able to tour England, attend the wedding, and spend almost a full month in the United States before returning to Israel.

Rabbi Povarski looked surprised at my request. How could I leave yeshiva a few days early? After all, the *zman* was still in session.

"But *Rebbe,*" I retorted, "it's already after Purim, and I'm only leaving three days before *Rosh Chodesh Nissan.*" Then I added what I thought would be the convincing argument. "Anyway, it is not the middle of the *zman* — it's the end of the *zman.*"

Rav Povarski looked at me very sternly. Then he smiled dejectedly while shaking his head as if the situation were hopeless. "Back in Europe, in the Mir," he said, referring to one of the great Lithuanian *yeshivos,* "there was the *zman,* and there was *bain hazmanim.* That was all there was. It was either *zman* or not-*zman.* The Americans came and invented a new concept — the end of the *zman.*"

The Torah is teaching us the greatness of our leaders. They are always moving and exerting the most painstaking efforts to go forward. They may be about to tell us that it is all over, but until that moment they are still going forward, without faltering. The same enthusiasm that Moshe had in leading his people through the desert — the same vigor he had when ordering Pharaoh to let the Jews leave Egypt — was still with him until the last moments of his life. Until Moshe stopped —— Moshe went.

Parshas Ha'azinu

Non-Trivial Pursuit

The song of *Ha'azinu* encompasses a panoramic view of Jewish history, telling us of the past, present, and future of *Klal Yisrael.* However, Moshe did not end the portion with a song. Instead, he exhorted the Jews to take his words seriously and apply them to their hearts. Then he reiterated the most prevalent theme of all his teachings, saying, "Be careful to perform the entire Torah, for it is not an empty thing for you; for it is your life" *(Deuteronomy 32:46-47).*

The spectrum from "not an empty thing" to "it is your life" is extremely broad. Therefore, it is quite disconcerting to see Moshe proclaim to the nation he had guided with words of Torah that Torah is not an empty thing. Can he have meant something deeper?

Rashi tells us that Moshe, in fact, did mean something far more significant, for there is no empty thing in Torah. Every fact, no matter how small, bears enormous relevance; even the seemingly trivial fact in *Sefer Braishis,* "the sister of Lotun was Timna" (*Genesis 36:22*), is a springboard for philosophical, historical, and even kabalistic discussions.

Once again, something needs clarification. The Torah tells us that there is not one empty, irrelevant, and trivial thing in the Torah, as it is your life. Yet is there no middle ground? Can something be important yet not be life-encompassing?

When I was in seventh grade, one of my classmates was frustrated by a difficult commentary that Rashi cites. "I don't like this Rashi," the student quipped.

My *Rebbe,* Rabbi Shmuel Dishon, stopped him short with a story that had occurred to his fabled friend Chaim.

Chaim was on a tour of Paris' Louvre. On the tour, there also was an elderly American woman, whose appreciation for art must have begun and ended with her grandchildren's works hanging proudly on her refrigerator. As the guide passed the Mona Lisa, the oohs and ahs of the crowd were drowned out by the woman's cynicism.

"Is she smiling or not smiling? Can't Da Vinci make up his mind?" she *kvetched.* The Rembrandts and Reubens did not escape her criticisms, either.

When the guide began to explain distinctive painting styles, the differences of oils and brush-strokes, and a host of other amazing facts and analyses, the women let out a sigh of impatience. "I really don't see what is so wonderful about these pictures! My grandson..."

The guide cut her short. In perfect, French-accented English, he began, "My dear madam, when you go to the Louvre, you must realize the paintings are no longer on trial. They have already been scrutinized and analyzed by those who have spent their entire lives studying art. Every stroke of the brush has been critiqued and praised. What hangs here are the standard-bearers for every generation of artists to come.

"No, my dear woman," he continued, "at the Louvre, the paintings are not on trial. It is *you* who are on trial. The paintings have passed the test. It is you who have failed."

Needless to say, my classmate understood our *Rebbe*'s point.

In order to appreciate every item in the Torah, and to understand that every fact, figure, and seemingly trivial detail contains endless depth and countless meanings, one must make the Torah his life. Here, then, Moshe is giving us more than a critique of Torah wisdom; he is instead teaching us a fundamental Torah principle: "There is not one empty thing in Torah when it is your life!"

If a person makes a serious career of Torah study, if he analyzes it, and commits himself to Torah knowledge, then he will be amazed at the never-ending lessons, laws, and lifestyle-improvements he will glean from it.

Imagine, in 1637, French mathematician Pierre de Fermat wrote a tiny theorem, "The equation $x^n + y^n = z^n$ where n is an integer greater than 2 has no solution in positive integers." In the margin of his copy of a work by Diophantus, a Greek mathematician, he noted that he had found a truly wonderful proof which that space was too small to contain.

For 350 years, in universities around the world, mathematicians toiled unsuccessfully to decipher his riddle. And in June of 1993, *The New York Times* shouted, "Eureka," to what may have finally been a solution, quoting mathematicians who called it, "the most exciting thing that's happened, — maybe ever, in mathematics!" For those who live math, it is their life, and they live to fit in the missing pieces of what may seem to many of us as insignificant mathematical minutia.

I recall my years in yeshiva, a very different world where the triumphs and enthusiasm of finding new explanations are reveled in daily.

Our teachers quoted the great sage of Israel, Rabbi Akiva Eiger, who, *lehavdil*, a term denoting clear demarcation from anything secular, also wrote very brief questions and comments on the sides his Talmud, often ending his notations with the words, "there is no room to elaborate."

My great teachers would spend hours upon hours, sometimes a few days' worth of *shiurim*, to find the answers and explanations that eluded Reb Akiva Eiger's quill, ink, and parchment! And the enthusiasm and rejoicing in deciphering his words occurs daily. And though not noted in *The New York Times*, the excitement is surely noted in the celestial spheres of eternal wisdom. For surely, the everlasting words of the Torah contain theorems that sustain us eternally. And they are to be found in the tiniest details. We must, however, actively pursue them. And when we are truly in pursuit of truth, we will find that the Torah contains nothing trivial.

PARSHAS V'ZOS HABRACHA

Terms of Endearment

God's eulogy for Moshe should consist of the most poetic words known to man to describe an individual who fulfilled Hashem's every wish and command incumbent upon mortal beings. Indeed, in summarizing Moshe's life's achievements, He should have chosen words that describe Moshe's remarkable humility, his unstinting devotion, and his amazing powers of reason and sensibility. Hashem didn't.

"And Moshe, the *eved* Hashem (servant of God), died" *(Deuteronomy* 34:5). "*Eved* Hashem" are the two words chosen to encapsulate the life of the greatest man in Biblical history. Just two simple words — *servant of God.* Do these words do Moshe justice? How could such a simple compliment, calling the Torah's greatest prophet a simple servant, help us understand God's praise for his greatest disciple?

Fredrick the Great, King of Prussia during the late 1700s, was reviewing his troops when he noticed a middle-aged soldier wearing an interesting ornament. Dangling from what appeared to be an heirloom watch-chain was a bullet. It had been polished and shined, as it replaced a watch that the soldier was obviously unable to afford.

The king, in a playful mood, pulled his diamond-studded pocket watch from his vest and held it in the sunlight. As the rays glinted off the diamonds that surrounded its face, he stared intently at his time-

piece. Then he looked at the soldier. "My dear man," he said in mock concern, as he tugged on the exquisite watch attached to its chain, "my timepiece says that it is half-past one. What time does yours tell?"

The soldier looked down at the bullet.

"Your Honor," he declared with sincere humility. "The ornament that dangles from my watch chain does not tell me the time. Rather, it is a bullet."

"A bullet!" scoffed the king. "Why on earth would you wear a bullet instead of a watch?"

"To me, your honor, there are no hours, minutes, or seconds. My watch tells me that every moment I am willing to take a bullet — even if it means my life — for your Majesty."

King Fredrick was so impressed with the soldier's reply that he promptly removed his exquisite royal watch and presented it to the soldier.

Mortals look for accolades that authenticate their own wisdom, wealth, and accomplishment. The Torah, however, looks for accomplishments that confirm a man's reason for being.

The greatest praise that the Creator can bestow upon His beloved are two Hebrew words — *eved* Hashem — Servant of God. Moshe was completely subservient to the will of his Creator, making himself a mortal extension of His immortal directives. Those two words — *eved* Hashem — say a great deal. They tell us more than hundreds of pages of eulogy and praise or tomes of accolades. They give the *raison d'être* of mortal man — to serve Hashem.

As we ponder our existence, it's wonderful to remember those words, for they help us focus on the true meaning of life while keeping its complexities simple. All we have to desire is to reach that great level of simplicity. For the greatest level of simplicity is often the highest level of honor. If we bear in mind that our goal in life is to reach the Creator, then His service is the greatest achievement we can strive for.

ימים טובים

Holidays

Rosh Hashana

Identity Crisis

Throughout the liturgy of our holidays, we find references to the Almighty in varying expressions. He is called Our Creator, The Compassionate One, The Master of all Powers, and a host of other names, each describing a different facet of His all-encompassing essence.

But there are two characteristics that seem to go in tandem quite often, and this association needs explanation. The expression is mentioned most often in the prayer we say for ten days beginning at *Rosh Hashana* (except when it falls on *Shabbos*), after both *Shacharis* and *Mincha* (morning and afternoon) services. In that prayer, *Avinu Malkeinu,* we refer to Hashem as "Our Father, Our King" no less than eighteen times. Such repetition gives us reason to reflect. If we are pleading with the Almighty as a father, and He is coincidentally our King — a fact that is known to all — then why mention it? Often, we separate the two attributes. We say in the *tefilah,* "If we are like sons, have mercy like a father on a son: and if we are like servants to a master, then our eyes are turned to You until You have mercy on us."

It seems from that *tefilah* that the love directed to a son is different than that for a subject. Why, then, in the prayer of *Avinu Malkeinu* are these two different attributes combined as one?

The Dubno Maggid tells the story of Velvel, a *cheder* teacher in a small *shtetl.* Velvel was a loving man who was known to be a kind and compassionate father who spent all his extra time with his family. As the only teacher in town, he also had an admirable reputation as an instructor whose students excelled at

their work. But there was one aspect of his classroom comportment that all the children learned very quickly. He began each year as a strict disciplinarian. If a boy did not behave, he was not spared the wrath of the back of the teacher's hand. Velvel did not *"potch"* often, but if he did, he would almost never have to discipline a student again.

One year, Reb Velvel was in a dilemma. His son, Yankele, was entering his class, and Reb Velvel knew that as long as his boy was in the classroom, he himself would have to lay aside his gentle demeanor and treat his son, who had a reputation for misbehavior, as strictly as everyone else.

Before the first day of school, Velvel called Yankele to his small room and sat him down. "Yankele," he began softly, "tomorrow we begin *cheder.* I am your *Rebbe,* and I expect you to behave. You have to realize that as long as we are in the classroom together, I am your teacher. Do not call me Daddy, because I will not respond. I will treat you no differently than any boy in the class."

Yankele became very nervous, but his father continued. "But the moment school is over, you don't have to fear a thing. I will be just as warm and loving as I always am." And with that, Reb Velvel gave his son a hug and a kiss and sent him out to play.

The next morning school began, and it did not take long before Yankele began to act in a rowdy manner. Reb Velvel walked up to his seat and without warning landed a *potch* on his soft pink cheek. For the rest of the day, Yankele acted like an angel.

After school was let out, Yankele was running toward his home when he noticed his father, too, walking slowly in the same direction. The boy caught up with the older man and walked slowly behind him.

Then with fatherly affection, Reb Velvel turned to his son. "So, Yankele, how was your first day of *cheder?"* he asked with a broad smile.

Yankele sighed. "It was okay." Then he turned to his father and with tears welling in his eyes he added,

"But, Papa could you please do me a favor?"

"Surely my son!" responded Reb Velvel.

The boy began to sob. "Please tell the *Rebbe* not to *potch* me any more!"

On *Rosh Hashanah,* we acknowledge the many attributes of the Almighty. But we ask our heavenly Father never to ignore that most compassionate characteristic, no matter which other he embraces. Because even if he is Our King, Our Creator, and Our Master, we are secure — because he is still Our Father!

Yom Kippur

Repent Now — Avoid The Rush

As a youngster, I remember my teachers comparing *Yom Kippur* to the last game of an important baseball series, and the final supplications of *Ne'eilah* to the proverbial situation of bottom of the ninth, bases loaded, two outs, full count.

I suppose that trivializing the most important day of the year by comparing it to a ball game works — at least for grade-schoolers. But the comparisons are also there on different levels, whether they are to closing gates, or a setting sun, for after *Yom Kippur,* the game is truly almost over.

And so, on the *Shabbos* prior to *Yom Kippur,* we read a special *Haftorah* which stresses the importance of penitence and the urgency of the moment. The *Haftorah* portion begins with the words, *Shuva Yisrael.* So significant are those words that the entire *Shabbos* is named for them: *Shabbos Shuva!*

The verse reads, "*Shuva Yisrael ahd Hashem Elokecha.* Repent, Israel, unto Hashem, for you have stumbled in your sins" (*Hosea 14:1*). It is interesting to note that the word *ahd,* generally translated as unto, can actually mean until.

The commentaries note that and are concerned: "What does the prophet mean, repent *until* Hashem? It sounds as if the prophet is telling us to repent up until we reach Hashem. Is it possible that the word until denotes that something should transpire before we actually reach Hashem?

The farmer's son grew up in the field. In fact, he was raised as if he were one of the livestock, taught no manners, table or otherwise, versed in no rules of

etiquette. He ate with his hands, and did not know the meaning of the words please or thank you.

When the boy was fourteen years old, his father realized that the child would have to go to the city to receive an education. As such, the man decided to send his son out of town, to live with an uncle, where he would attend a proper school and receive a decent education.

The farmer also knew that his son would never be able to function within a family setting without a crash course in social behavior. And so the farmer began teaching his child what he should have taught him over the previous fourteen years.

"When you arrive, you shake hands and say, 'It is so nice to meet you!' Every morning, you greet people with, 'Good morning,' and at night you say, 'Good evening.'"

"Remember," the man continued, "'The meal was delicious!' 'Yes, please, I would love some more!' 'No, thank you!' 'Yes, sir.'"

For the next four weeks, the boy repeated the sayings verbatim. Indeed, he did so well that he had it down to a science.

But when he arrived at his uncle's home, he was shocked to see a beautiful mansion with a footman at the door! As the entire family stood in the background, the uncle greeted him with outstretched arms and a broad smile!

"How are you my nephew? How was your trip?"

The boy's nervous response was the product of a four-week crash course in etiquette. In a nervous ramble, he began to chant, "The trip was wonderful, it is so nice to meet you. Good morning. Good evening. The meal was delicious! Yes, please, I would love some more! No, thank you! Yes, sir! Have a good day!"

Perhaps the *posuk* is actually warning us to do *teshuva before* we reach the final at-bat. It warns us to be careful, calculated, and methodical in our process, realizing way before it is too late to repent with a clear mind and organized process. Of course, the

Navi says that you can repent up to the point when Hashem is standing in front of you about to close the door at *Ne'ilah*. But in order to avoid the rush, try to do it until you get there!

The prophet tells us, "Repent, until you come to face Hashem your God!" Often, we cram everything into the waning hours of *Yom Kippur.* And though Hashem greets us then, too, with open arms, our response should not be babbled, compressed, and confused! We have ample time — an entire year — the month of *Elul* — *Rosh Hashana* — to repent. Let's beat the rush!

SUKKOS

Nobody is a Somebody

One of the most joyous customs associated with the holiday of *Sukkos* is the celebration of *Simchas Bais Hashoaevah*. In the times of the *Bais HaMikdash*, a water libation ceremony accompanied the customary holiday offerings. *Simchas Bais Hashoaevah,* literally, the Joy of the Water Drawing, was observed with a most ebullient celebration. It included a marvelously varied array of harps, lyres, cymbals, and trumpets, among other instruments. The greatest sages and most pious rabbis performed acrobatics and antics that would have normally been beneath their dignity. In fact, the sages in Tractate *Sukkah* note that, "One who has not seen the celebration of the *Bais Hashoaevah* has never seen true joy."

Rambam (Maimonides) discusses this aspect of exuberance and adds that, "One who in his insolence restrains himself from serving Hashem in a joyous manner is a sinner and fool." Yet *Rambam* adds a caveat. "But this joy was not performed by the ignorant ones and by anyone who wanted (to dance). Only the great sages of Israel, the heads of *yeshivos* and the *Sanhedrin,* the pious, the elders, and men of righteous action would dance, clap, and sing in the *Bais HaMikdash* on *Sukkos*. Everyone else, men and women, would come to watch and listen" (*Hilchos Lulav 8:14*).

This begs explanation. Why shouldn't *everyone,* even the most profane of men, sing and dance and make merry in celebration of the Lord? Further, what does *Rambam* mean by not including "those who want to dance?" Ultimately, anyone who ended up dancing, even the most pious sages, obviously wanted to dance. What, then, does *Rambam* mean when he says that this joy was not performed by simply anyone who wanted to dance?

A classic story circulates in virtually all Jewish humor anthologies:

Before the start of the *Ne'eilah* service, the holiest and final supplication of Yom Kippur, the rabbi rose from his seat and bolted toward the Holy Ark. He spread his hands toward heaven and cried out, "*Ribbono Shel Olam*, Master of the Universe, I am a total nothing before You! Please inscribe me in the Book of Life!"

All of a sudden, the *chazzan* ran toward the *aron* and joined the rabbi! "Almighty Father," he shouted, "please forgive me, too, for I am truly a nothing before You!"

There was an awed silence among the congregants.

The *shammas* then followed suit. He, too, ran up toward the ark, and in tearful supplication pronounced, "I, too, am a nothing!"

Mouths around the congregation dropped open. The president of the synagogue's men's club, Ed Goldstein, was also caught up in the fervor of the moment. Suddenly, he, too, bolted from his seat in the back and lumbered toward the front of the *shul.* With great eagerness he prostrated himself in front of the ark and cried out at the top of his lungs. "Forgive me, oh Lord," he shouted, "for I, too, am a nothing!"

Suddenly, an incredulous shout from the back of the synagogue was directed toward Goldstein's bent figure.

"Harrumph!" the man said. "Who is Goldstein to be a nothing?"

Rambam teaches us that whoever runs to dance and sing and make crazy is not truly lowering himself before the Almighty. And if someone inherently likes to cavort wildly, then he is not dancing for the sake of lowering himself before the Almighty; rather, he is having a wonderful time. When King David brought the Holy Ark to Jerusalem, he danced in front of it as if he were a lowly slave. When confronted by his wife, Michal for dancing like a servant, he retorted, "I would make myself even lower before Hashem" (see *Samuel II, Chapter* 6).

When rejoicing during the festivities, we must bear in mind our true reasons for enthusiasm: who we are, and why we dance. Because in order to be a nobody, first you have to be a somebody.

Simchas Torah

Making It by Breaking It

We celebrate the holiday of *Simchas Torah* by dancing with the Torah that we are about to conclude. And then the entire congregation gathers in anticipation, as we read the final verses, all poised in unison to shout the triumphant cry of encouragement and continuity, "*Chazak, Chazak, V'nischazaik!* Be strong, be strong, and we shall strengthen each other!"

But in those moments of anticipation, perhaps we forget to analyze the last sentences of the Torah. And perhaps they send a message to all Jews who follow Hashem's words though the guidance of the *Chachamim.*

In a few brief sentences, the last verses of the Torah encapsulate the glorious leadership career of the father of all prophets, Moshe. "Never has there risen in Israel a prophet as Moshe, whom Hashem had known face to face; as apparent by all the signs and wonders that Hashem had sent him to perform in the land of Egypt against Pharaoh, and all his courtiers, and all his land; and by the strong hand and awesome power that Moshe performed before the eyes of Israel" *(Deuteronomy 34:10-12).*

While it's a powerful descriptive, the words are as cryptic as they are awe-inspiring. What is the "strong hand" and that Moshe performed before the eyes of all Israel? Does it refer to the horrific plagues brought on Egypt? Perhaps it refers to splitting the sea or opening the earth to swallow Korach and his rebellious cohorts?

Rashi tells us that the words, "Moshe performed before the eyes of Israel," refer to something completely different, perhaps very mortal. Rashi explains that the posuk refers to Moshe descending Mount Sinai, seeing the nation dancing before the Golden Calf, then smashing the Tablets. As such, Rashi quotes the verse, "and I smashed the Tablets before your eyes" (*Deuteronomy 9*).

Rashi's comment evokes many questions. Why is smashing the Luchos mentioned as an awe-inspiring feat? More important, is this the final way to remember Moshe — as the man who smashed the Luchos? Is that the appropriate parting descriptive of Judaism's greatest leader?

I remember my grandfather, Rabbi Yaakov Kamenetzky, of blessed memory, telling me the following story. Since that time, I have heard numerous variations, some that I have incorporated into this version.

Rabbi Yisrael Lipkin of Salant was Rav in the city when a typhus epidemic erupted. Despite the peril of the contagious disease, Rabbi Lipkin went together with a group of his students to aid the sick, making sure they had food and clothing. In addition, the roving first-aid committee imposed strict restrictions upon the townsfolk, imploring them to eat properly every day in order to ward off immunological deficiencies.

With *Yom Kippur* quickly approaching, Rabbi Lipkin decreed that due to the epidemic, absolutely no one was permitted to fast on *Yom Kippur*, despite it being required on the holiest day of the year.

The town's elders were skeptical, for they felt that Rabbi Salanter had no right to impose such a ruling on those who were not afflicted. Yet despite their protestations, Rabbi Salanter was unfazed. In fact, he made his point in a very dramatic way.

On *Yom Kippur* morning, immediately after the shacharis services, he went up to the *bimah*, made *kiddush*, drank wine, and ate a piece of cake!

Immediately, the townsfolk were relieved. They went to their homes and followed suit.

The elders were outraged at this seemingly blatant violation of Jewish tradition. When they

approached Rabbi Lipkin to protest his disregard for the sanctity of the day, Rabbi Lipkin remained adamant.

"I have taken a group of students for the last month," he said, "and together we have attended to scores of typhus victims. Before we went out, though, I guaranteed every mother that each child will return home healthy. So it is on my guarantee that not one of those students became ill!"

He turned to the elders and declared. "When you are able to make such guarantees, then you can tell me the laws against eating on *Yom Kippur*!"

When the Torah ends with the greatness of Moshe, it refers to his accomplishments as his *Yad haChazaka,* his strong hand before the eyes of Israel — breaking the two tablets. Like Rabbi Lipkin, Moshe's greatness was not only knowing how to accept the Ten Commandments, but also knowing when to smash them. And though not every one of us is equipped with the ability to overrule a Jewish practice or tradition, *Klal Yisrael* knows that when the time to act is upon us, our great ones will arise to build by smashing what needs to be broken.

Whether it is breaking a fast or breaking the tablets, it takes a great man to understand the time to build — and an even greater man to know the time to tear down.

Chanukah

The Rest of the Story

It's quite interesting that the holiday that celebrates the victory over the Greco-Syrian empire, entailing fierce and often bloody battles, is formed from a conjunction of two words that denote passivity: *Chanu — kah,* they rested on the 25th.

The name does not denote that they were victorious on the 25th, nor does it mean we crushed them on the 25th. It means that the Jews, namely the Hasmoneans, rested on the 25th.

The question is simple. Why name a holiday "we rested"? Shouldn't the celebration's titular inference depict the struggles and the victory, rather than calm and rest?

On the fast day of the Tenth of *Teves,* during the height of World War II, Rabbi Ahron Kotler took the well known activist Irving Bunim on a train trip to Washington. The war in Europe was raging, Jews were being exterminated, and the two had to see a high-ranking government official to plead with him in every possible way — "save our brothers!" On the way down to Washington, Rabbi Kotler tried to persuade Bunim to break his fast.

"Bunim," he explained. "You cannot fast now. You need your strength for the meeting."

But Irving Bunim refused to eat. He was sure that he could hold out until the evening when the fast ended.

The meeting was intense. Rabbi Kotler cried, cajoled, and begged the official to respond. Finally, the great rabbi felt that he had impressed upon the man the gravity of the situation. The man gave his

commitment that he would talk to the President. When they left the meeting, Bunim was exhausted. He mentioned to Rabbi Kotler that he thought the meeting went well and now he'd like to eat.

Rav Ahron was quick to reply. "With Hashem's help it will be good. And Bunim," he added, "*now* you can fast!"

In Jewish life there is no such thing as rest. Rest is just a preparation for the next battle. It is a time to garner our strength, fortify our resources, and prepare for the next accomplishment. *Chanukah* was not a total rest — merely one rest from one battle. The Hasmoneans had to rededicate the desecrated Temple, relight the *Menorah,* and re-establish the supremacy of Torah over a Hellenist culture that had corrupted Jewish life. They rested from physical battle, but they knew that it was a rejuvenation respite for the constant battle over spirituality for ages to come.

The way they rested was by establishing the *Menorah*-lighting ceremony with flames that have glowed until today, proclaiming with each flicker that the battle may be over but the war is endless.

PURIM

Happy Purim — Whatever that Means...

First a *Purim* story. Humorist Leo Rosten told of the Nifkowitz family, who made a fortune and moved to Oyster Bay. To fit in, they changed their name to Northridge and soon were invited to join a prestigious country club. And there, at a charity event, a waiter spilled hot soup right in the lap of Mrs. Northridge. *"Gevalt!"* she exclaimed, "whatever that means!"

The original *Purim* story ended on a happy note. The Jews were spared, the villain hung, the enemies defeated, and our leaders exalted. And for the simple folks — the Jewish nation that was spared annihilation? Well, the *Megillah* tells us that they, too, walked away from the would-be tragedy with something. "For the Jews there was light, joy, happiness, and splendor" (*Esther 8:15*). Sounds good enough. After all, we all could use a little enlightenment, joy, happiness, and splendor. Why not?

But that's not good enough for the Talmudic sages. Not that they had something against light, joy, happiness, and splendor; it's just that they have a different take on them. The Talmud in Tractate *Megillah* expounds: "Light means Torah, gladness means *bris milah,* joy means *Yom Tov,* and splendor means *tefillin."* The blaring question is why does the simple meaning not suffice? What concerns our sages to elevate joy from simple celebration to lofty idealism?

At the great stadium in Moscow, back in the mid-1970's, Chairman Leonoid Brezhnev was addressing a large audience filled with the Communist Party faithful.

"By the year 2000," he declared, "every family in the Soviet Union will have its own airplane!"

The crowd roared with sheer exhilaration!

Suddenly a small voice emerged from the great throng, "Mr. Premier!" he shouted "Mr. Premier! I do not understand! Why would a family in Moscow need an airplane?"

All of a sudden, a great hush overtook the crowd. There was stone silence. Then from nowhere a voice boomed. "You fool! Of course you'll need an airplane! Maybe there will be potatoes in Kiev!"

The Talmud is not satisfied with joy just meaning joy, or happiness meaning smiley faces and have-a-nice-day bumper stickers. The *Gemara* feels that the Jews were celebrating a reclamation of things more spiritual than a smile.

Happiness is meaningless unless we have a good spiritual reason for it. Joy, enlightenment, and splendor have no value if they cannot attach to permanent holiness.

Before the FCC liberated Americans from most tobacco advertising back in the early 1970s, cigarette manufacturers spent millions trying to convince us that happiness was the taste of a particular cigarette. Today, in smoke-free environments, they are still attempting to convince us what joy is.

It seems that the world at large is confused. There are no clear definitions, because yesterday's joy is today's unfulfillment. The *Megillah* wrote that the Jews had happiness and splendor, but the sages knew that there must have been more than mere parties and passing whims. If happiness were only the revelry of a fleeting moment, then *Purim* would have been at most a local celebration — and lost in history. The *Megillah* itself would never have made the astonishing prediction that the holiday of *Purim* shall never pass from the Jewish nation, nor will the story ever be forgotten! It knew that the enlightening aspect of *Purim,* that was destined to last eternally, must be linked to true eternity.

Enlightenment is Torah! The joy that is to last forever must be intrinsically linked to a joy that waxes eternal! Joy is *bris milah.* Happiness that just ends in drinks and partying is as ludicrous as giving people airplanes to find potatoes! As such, *Purim* celebrations must be special. Our joy must manifest itself in helping the poor. Our food and drink should include those less fortunate. Our *shalach manos* baskets should contain more meaning than the gift items placed inside. Indeed, if you are looking for happiness without any spiritual meaning, your joy will just go up in smoke.

PESACH

Life, Liberty and The Pursuit of Matzah

Did it ever concern you that the symbolic food of freedom, the so-called bread that never rose as we fled the land of Egypt, is a poor symbol of freedom? After so many years of servitude, shouldn't the Jews indulge in something more rich? Perhaps, as we lean the night of the *Seder,* we should savor seven-layer-cake instead of crunching brittle *matzah?* Wouldn't an elaborate pastry filled with all sorts of delicious treats best represent freedom? Why must we eat the simplest and most impoverished of all foods? Even the Torah calls it *Lechem Oni,* poor man's bread.

Why then does it also represent our freedom?

There is a beautiful story told about a king whose daughter was deathly ill. His sorcerers advised him that the only cure would be for his daughter to wear the jacket of the happiest man in the kingdom. Naturally, the servants, who were sent to find this individual, first approached the wealthiest banker in the Kingdom.

"Happy?" he sighed. "Wealthy I am. But how can I be happy when I have no time to spend with my family? I have all the money in the world, but time, I have not a moment to spare. It would be untrue if I were to claim that I am truly happy."

The servants approached lawyers, doctors, and businessmen. Each one felt that he was very successful, but doubted that in spite of his wealth he could be characterized the happiest man in the kingdom.

The servants were advised to visit a certain very poor woodcutter. Though he could barely feed his children, he was always smiling and singing as he labored, chopping wood.

"Happy?" he responded, "why I'm always happy. The good Lord has bestowed upon me only a bounty of blessing. I have a wonderful wife and beautiful children! I am healthy, and the sun shines for me each day! I have not a worry in the world! I bet you that I am the happiest man in this entire kingdom. Why do you ask?"

The king's servants could not contain themselves. "We've been looking for a person like you for the last few weeks. We need your jacket! The king needs your jacket! His daughter needs your jacket! Her life depends on it!"

Puzzled, the poor man looked back at them with despair. "I'd love to help the king and his daughter," he said. "However, I can not. You see, I don't even own a jacket."

Imagine a luscious cake with all sorts of ingredients. Besides the flour, eggs, and water, it has butter, sugar, and an array of spices. It also needs leavening agents, baking soda, and baking powder — all necessary to make it the perfect masterpiece. If even one ingredient is left out, you may have a cake — but it will not taste like one. Every ingredient depends on several others to make it work. The successful outcome is dependent on many small factors, from the texture to the mixture to the oven temperature. It has no independence.

Matzah, on the other hand, is solely dependent on the two ingredients that comprise its very essence — flour and water. It needs no additives, no flavorings or emulsifiers. It may not be rich, but it is free.

We often confuse wealth with freedom and poverty with servitude. Actually, one has nothing to do with the other — and the two may even be incongruous! Freedom is the ability to exist on our own without dependence or worry. How often do people with many assets suffer sleepless nights because everything is tied up in their portfolio? They are tied to their lawyers, accountants, and fax-machines! The simple unpretentious man, however, is not tied to anything. He lives in his humble abode, supports himself with the few cents he earns, and is satisfied with his simple life. He may not be rich, but he is free.

Rabbi Yehuda Lowy of Prague, better known as the *Maharal,* explains that the message of *matzah* is one that is reiterated throughout the Talmud. "The free man is one who is involved in Torah." The restrictions of the Torah are not obstructive. Instead, they give a sense of freedom in which one can control his will and say, "I won't eat that," "I won't go there," "I won't be tempted." He, then, is truly in control, as opposed to those who say, "I must wear that," or "I must eat that," or "I must see that," because a French or Italian chef, or Hollywood critic, so advises. Like the *matzah,* as life is simplified so are your desires, dreams, and dependencies. You focus on what you really want, not on a list of ingredients that has no connection to your true essence. That is true freedom.

Shavuos

Transcending Celebration

A unique aspect of the holiday of *Shavuous* struck me as I was explaining the customs of the holidays to some beginners. They began to review the various holiday laws with me. "OK," began one young man. "So on *Pesach* you've got the *matzah,* and the *mitzvah* of telling the story of the Exodus." "Correct," I nodded. "And on *Sukkos* you've got the *lulav, esrog* and eating in a *sukkah* the entire holiday — right."

Again I gave an approving nod and smiled. The student continued.

"And what special observance does the Torah tell us to do on *Shavuos?*"

I hesitated. Sacrifices aside, what special *mitzvah* observance do we do to commemorate the receiving of the Torah?

In fact, the Torah tells us in *Parshas Re'eh* how we celebrate the holiday.

"You shall count seven-weeks for yourselves ... Then you shall observe the holiday of *Shavuos* for Hashem ... You shall rejoice before Hashem, you, your son, your daughter, your servant, your maidservant, the Levite in your cities, the proselyte, the orphan and the widow who are among you" (*Deuteronomy 16:9-11*).

I was reluctant to respond with, "we stay up all night and learn" or "we eat blintzes at the holiday meal," — beautiful customs that are in no way comparable to the level of a Torah-ordained command.

Why is there no physical act in commemoration of the *Yom Tov*? There is no Torah-prescribed requirement to blow *shofar,* read a special Torah portion (the reading of the Ten Commandments is Rabbinically ordained), or special ritual to commemorate the event. There is only all-inclusive rejoicing.

Why is joy the only way to celebrate? And why is every type of citizen mentioned? Aren't the poor and rich, widowed and orphaned included in every command?

When my grandfather, Rabbi Yaakov Kamenetzky, of blessed memory, passed away, his student, Rabbi Yitzchok Chinn, of Gemilas Chesed Congregation of McKeesport, Pennsylvania, eulogized him at the end of the *shloshim* period of mourning. He related the following story:

In the early 1950s Reb Yaakov spent his summers at Camp Mesivta in Ellenville, NY. One summer, a young boy asked Reb Yaakov a most difficult question, "*Rebbe,*" he inquired, "where is my *neshama* (soul)?"

Reb Yaakov turned to the boy and asked him, "Where is your arm?"

The boy stuck out his arm.

"Good!" said Reb Yaakov. "I want you to shake it."

The boy began to shake his arm up and down. Reb Yaakov smiled, "Good. Who does that arm belong to?"

The young boy continued shaking his arm while answering. "It belongs to me of course!"

"Good," responded Reb Yaakov. "Now shake your other arm." The boy began flapping his other arm."

"Wonderful! Now show me your leg. " The boy lifted his foot. "Now shake it!"While continuing to flap his arms, the boy shook his leg. "Who does the leg belong to?"

Again the boy laughed, "Why to me, of course!"

Then Reb Yaakov smiled. "Now your other leg!" The boy began to jump and shake and rock and sway. And as he watched the youngster move with every part of his very essence, Reb Yaakov gave him a tremendous smile and exclaimed, "All of these parts, to who do they belong?" Jumping in glee the boy shouted, "THEY BELONG TO ME!!"

Reb Yaakov smiled. "But who does ME belong to?" then he paused and exclaimed, "That is your *neshama!*"

The only way to commemorate the receiving of the Torah is to celebrate the receipt of our nation's soul. We cannot celebrate the soul with a physical commemoration. The soul of the nation celebrates by shaking every one of its parts — poor or rich, wealthy or poor, free or slave, son or daughter — with unmitigated joy.

The only way to capture the essence of our very being and our gratitude for the gift that infused us with boundless spirituality is through a rejoicing that permeates every part of the Jewish body; its arms, legs, and torso — The Torah. The observance is not relegated to eating an item, telling a story, hearing a *shofar* or sitting in a booth. Like the Torah we received, the celebration encompasses every aspect of our lives. And that is done thorough joyous *simcha.*

TISHA B'AV

Unquestioned Answers

Recently, the expression that Jews traditionally wished each other before the start of the *Tisha B'Av* fast was replaced by what one might call a more evocative one. What was once "have an easy fast" has been transformed into "have a meaningful fast." While "easy" or "meaningful" are not necessarily contradictory, nevertheless in order to make any fast meaningful, we first must understand why we are fasting. And in order to understand why we are fasting, we must think. A good place to begin is a verse in *Eicha,* the *Book of Lamentations,* composed by the prophet Yirmiyahu as he watched the Temple, and the society of his times, erode and crumble, and the Jewish people go into exile.

Despite suffering a terrible fate, seeing his leaders, his beloved people, and his cherished Temple all destroyed, he tells the nation: "Of what shall a living man complain? A strong man for his sins! Let us search and examine our ways, and return to Hashem" *(Lamenetations* 3:39-40).

The prophet's question, "Of what shall a living man complain?" is difficult to understand. People always complain. Didn't Yirmiyahu experience enough to complain about? Also why does Yirmiyahu ask about a living man? Dead men don't tell tales, and they don't complain either. So why the extra word?

Perhaps the second question answers the first, and the second verse emphasizes the answer.

The Chasam Sofer once met a very old man and asked him the secret of his longevity.

"I know that long life is a gift," the great sage said. "Tell me, what exemplary act did you do that merited you these long years?"

The old man looked up and smiled. "Actually, I did nothing special. You see I have a different theory about long life. I stuck to my theory, and it worked for me."

"And what is that theory?" the great sage inquired.

The old man wrinkled his deeply lined face. " Like myself, all my friends went through their share of *tzorus* and misfortunes. We all do. They are, however, not here any longer. I am."

"But why?" prodded the Chasam Sofer. "That was exactly my question. What is the secret of your longevity? Yes! We all have our *tzorus.* But they didn't break you! You are still alive and in very good health. What is the difference between you and your friends?"

"You see," answered the old man, "my friends asked 'Why?' I, however, did not."

The Chasam Sofer seemed puzzled, but the man continued his monologue. "You see, every time tragedy struck, my friends would ask the Almighty, 'why did this happen? How did I come to deserve this?' They would plead and prod the Creator for answers that no mortal mind could understand. And you know what happened?"

The Chasam Sofer shook his head, careful not to interrupt the man's train of thought.

"Hashem said, 'Do you really want to understand? Come, I will show you.' And so He took them to a place where all the mysteries of life are revealed, a place where past and future collide and today's actions are the answers to history's expostulations."

The man continued. "I, on the other, hand, was not so curious. And if I was, I did not turn to Hashem and ask, 'Why?' Rather, I accepted what happened."

Then the man's face began to glow. "And do you know what? He never invited me upstairs to explain anything!"

Perhaps the essence of our annual mourning service can be summed up with Yirmiyahu's word's that analyze a mortal approach to immortal justice.

"Of what shall a living man complain? A strong man for his sins!" The prophet then answers his question. "Let us search and examine our ways, and return to Hashem."

We may have questions, but in essence they are not for us to find new answers. We are not to question *His* reasons. Instead, the only answer we can have is to search our *own* souls with introspection and return to Hashem.

In truth, we are not put in this world to demand answers. We are here to improve ourselves and, in essence, the world. And we are here to understand when to turn to our own lives for answers, instead of to the Almighty with questions, so that we may survive the tragedies with both faith and life intact.

Biographical Data

Alter, Rabbi Yehuda Leib (1847-1905) was a grandson of the Chidushei HaRim,who led the Chasidic dynasty of Gur and in essence all of Polish Jewry in his era. He authored *Sfas Emes* on the Pentateuch and on the Talmud and is known by that name.

Alter, Rabbi Simcha Bunim, (c. 1900-1992) led the Gerrer Chasidim through a period of unprecedented growth from the time he became Rebbe at age 80 until his passing in 1992. Known by the title of his *sefer, Laiv Simcha,* he was cherished for his insightful and fatherly guidance.

Alter, Rabbi Yisrael of Gur (1895-1977) was the son of the last Gerrer Rebbe in Europe, Rabbi Avraham Mordechai Alter. He re-established Gerrer *chasidus* in Israel and throughout the world after the decimation of Polish Jewry in the Holocaust. He is also known as the Bais Yisrael after the commentary he wrote with that title.

Alter, Rabbi Yitzchok Meir of Gur (1799-1866) founded the Gerrer Chasidic dynasty and author of the *Chidushei HaRim.* In addition to his chassidic leadership, he was recognized as a foremost Talmudic scholar.

Auerbach, Rabbi Shlomo Zalman (1910-1995) was one of the foremost Torah scholars of our generation. Dean of Yeshiva Kol Torah in Jerusalem, his *halachic* rulings guided thousands the world over.

Attar, Rabbi Chaim Ben see Ohr HaChaim

Baal Shem Tov, Rabbi Yisrael (1698-1760) was the founder of *chasidus.* He lived primarily in Medzhibozh but often traveled all over Eastern Europe to spread the message of *chasidus.* He had many disciples who became chasidic leaders.

Berditchev, Rabbi Levi Yitzchak 1740-1809) was a student of the Mezhricher Maggid and a widely revered chasidic leader. Author of *Kedushas Levi,* he is best known for his advocacy of all Jews.

Bunim, Irving (1903-1980) was an American Orthodox lay leader and teacher. A founder of the Young Israel movement, he played a prominent role in Holocaust rescue efforts on behalf of Va'ad Hatzalah. In his day, Irving Bunim's work on behalf of Torah Judaism was unequaled.

Chidushei HaRim, see Alter, Rabbi Yitzchok Meir of Gur

Chofetz Chaim (1838-1933) Rabbi Yisrael Meir HaKohen of Radin, was known by the title of his premier work on the laws of speech. Author of numerous books on Jewish law, including the classic *Mishnah B'rurah*, he was revered for his wisdom and piety.

Dubno Maggid (1741-1804) Rabbi Yaakov Kranz, was one of the most famous Maggidim of his era. His *drashos* were compiled into the classic homiletic work, *Ohel Yaakov*.

Dvinsk, Rabbi Meir Simcha HaKohen of, (1843-1926) was a brilliant talmudist, and Rav of the City of Dvinsk. He authored *Ohr Samayach* on the Rambam, and *Meshech Chochma* on the Chumash, which weaves myriad aspects of *drush* and Talmudic analysis, and is studied by every serious student of Torah.

Eibeschutz, Rabbi Y'honasan (1690-1764) was a brilliant talmudist, orator, rav, and kabbalist. A *Rosh Yeshiva* and Rav in Prague, among other cities, he authored scores of volumes on all aspects of Torah. Some of his most famous works are *Ya'aros D'vas*, a collection of major addresses, and *Urim V'Tumim* on *Shulchan Oruch*.

Eiger, Rabbi Akiva (1762-1838) was the Av Bais Din of Pozna. His classic compendium of responsa on the Talmud is required study for any serious Talmudic student. His genius was only surpassed by his great humility.

Eiger, Rabbi Leible (1816-1888) a student of his father Rabbi Shlomo, and grandfather, Rabbi Akiva Eiger, Reb Leible was drawn to chassidus and became a disciple of the chasidic dynasty of Kotzk. A brilliant Talmudist, Reb Leible, as he is known in chassididc circles, was revered by thousands of followers. He authored *Toras Emes* on Chumash and holidays.

Feinstein, Rabbi Moshe (1895-1986) was the *Rosh Yeshiva* of Mesivta Tiferes Yerushalayim in New York City and the leading halachic authority of his day. He authored *Igros Moshe* and *Dibros Moshe*, both classic works of responsa and Talmudic analysis.

Finkel, Rabbi Nosson Zvi (1849-1927) was the founder of both the Slobodka Yeshiva, in Lithuania, and the Chevron Yeshiva. Known as the Alter of Slobodka, he produced students who emerged as the rebuilders of Torah in the post-Holocaust era.

Gifter, Rabbi Mordechai (c.1917 -) is the *Rosh Yeshiva* of Telshe Yeshiva in Cleveland. Born in the United States, he studied in the Telshe Yeshiva in Europe, where he married the daughter of the Mashgiach, Rabbi Zalman Bloch. A member of the Moetzes Gedolei Torah, he is well known for his brilliant Talmudic analysis and inspiring oratory.

Grodzinsky, Rabbi Chaim Ozer (1863-1940), was Chief Rabbi of Vilna, Lithuania, and one of the leaders of world Jewry prior to the Holocaust.

Author of Achiezer, a classic of responsa literature, he regularly saw thousands who flocked to him to resolve complex halachic issues.

Igra, Rabbi Meshulom (1750-1803) was known for his brilliance in Torah scholarship even as a young child. At age seventeen he was appointed the Rav of Tisminitz and established a yeshiva where he established many students. He received and answered hundreds of questions in Jewish law from all over Europe, many published posthumously as *Sha'los V'Tshuvos Rav Meshulom Igra* and *Igra Ramah.*

Kagan, Rabbi Yisrael Meir HaCohen, see Chofetz Chaim.

Kahaneman, Rabbi Yosef Shlomo (1887–1969) was known as the Ponevezer Rav. A *Rosh Yeshiva* in Ponevez, Lithuania, Rav Kahaneman lost nearly his entire family in Europe, then resolved to rebuild in Israel. He built and headed the Ponevez Yeshiva, girls' and boys' yeshivos, an orphanage, and communities in B'nai B'rak and Ashdod.

Kamenetzky, Rabbi Yaakov (1891-1986, was Rav of Tzitivyan, Lithuania, and Toronto. A *Rosh Yeshiva* of Mesivta Torah Voda'ath and a member of the Moetzes Gedolei Torah, he was known for brilliant Torah solutions and advice in a wide array of matters. He authored *Emes L'Yaakov,* on Torah and the Talmud.

Kanievski, Rabbi Yakov Yisrael (1899-1985) was a brilliant Talmudist and leader of world Jewry. Belovedly known as the Steipler Gaon, and brother-in-law of the Chazon Ish, he authored *Kehillos Yaakov* on the Talmud. Rabbi Kanievski arrived in Israel in 1934, where he became *Rosh Yeshiva* of Bais Yosef Yeshiva and later Rosh Kollel of Kollel Chazon Ish.

Kaplan, Rabbi Mendel (1913-1985) was a student of Rabbi Elchanan Wassermann of Baranovitch, Poland. In 1965 he was appointed a Maggid Shiur at Talmudical Yeshiva of Philadelphia, where he was a rebbe to hundreds of students.

Kotler, Rabbi Ahron (1892-1962) the founder and *Rosh Yeshiva* of Beth Medrash Govoah of Lakewood, NJ. was a powerful force in the rebuilding of Torah in America. Formerly *Rosh Yeshiva* of Kletzk, Poland, his brilliant shiurim were published posthumously as *Mishnas Rav Ahron.*

Kranz, Rabbi Yaakov, see Dubno Maggid.

Levin, Rabbi Aryeh (1885-1969) was voluntary chaplain to the leper hospital and prisoners of the British Mandate in Palestine, where his saintly character earned him the admiration and love of thousands.

Lipkin, Rabbi Yisrael, of Salant (1810-1883) founded the *mussar* movement and served as *Rosh Yeshiva* in Rameilles and the Kovno Kollel. He was the author of *Ohr Yisrael.*

Lopian, Rabbi Eliyahu (1876-1970) was a *Rosh Yeshiva* in Kelm, Poland, and Yeshivas Chayai Olam in London before becoming the Mashgiach of Yeshivas K'far Chasidim, near Haifa.

Lowy, Rabbi Yehuda (1526-1609) was the Rabbi of Moravia, Posen, and Prague. Author of a vast array of Torah commentaries, the Maharal, as he is known, was one of the most influential figures in Jewish thought.

Malbim, Rabbi Meir Leibush (1800-1880) was the Rav of Wershna, Kampano and Bucharest among various cities. He was a prolific writer, expounding on every book of the Torah. In his battle against the tide of haskalah, his brilliant works were geared to prove authenticity of the Talmudic expostulations of the Torah's every word. A foremost grammarian, his works on *dikduk* (Biblical grammar) and Torah synonymy are unequaled.

Nachmanides (1194-1270) Rabbi Moshe ben Nachman of Gerona, Spain, was a prolific author and brilliant scholar who defended Judaism in the Christian debates at Barcelona. In addition to his masterful commentary on the Torah, he expounded a large portion of Talmud and Jewish philosophy.

Ohr HaChaim is the name of the commentary by Rabbi Chaim ben Atar (1696-1743) a famous kabalist, rabbi, and *Rosh Yeshiva* in Livorno, Italy. He moved to Jerusalem toward the end of his life and is buried there.

Ponevezer Rav, see Kahanaman, Rabbi Yosef Shlomo.

Povarski, Rabbi Dovid (1902-1998) was *Rosh Yeshiva* of Ponevez Yeshiva in B'nei Berak for nearly four decades. A student of the Mirrer Yeshiva and Rabbi Yeruchom Levovitz, Rabbi Povarski was a strict adherent of *mussar* teachings, as well as a brilliant *Rosh Yeshiva* who guided thousands of *talmidim.*

Rambam, (1135-1204) is the acronym for Rabbi Moshe ben Maimon a leading authority and author of the classic and comprehensive code of Jewish Law, *Mishne Torah.* Born in Spain, the Rambam left to Egypt where he was to the Sultan. In addition to his halachic works he wrote the classic *Moreh Nevuchim* on Jewish philosophy.

Rashi (1040-1105) Rabbi Shlomo Yitzchaki was the premier commentator on virtually every section of the Torah, Prophets, and Talmud. He headed one of the greatest Talmudic academies of his era in addition to maintaining a winery in southern France.

Salanter, Rabbi Yisrael of Salant, see Lipkin, Rabbi Yisrael of Salant

Schapira, Chaim Elazar, the Munkatcher Rebbe (d.1937) was a fiery leader of Hungarian Jewry during the period before World War II.

Author of the classical work of responsa, *Minchas Elozar* and a variety of other works on every aspect of Torah, he was known for his strong response to the enlightenment and strengthening his community during a most turbulent era.

Schwab, Rabbi Shimon (1908-1997) was a disciple of Rabbi Joseph Breuer, the Rav of the German K'hal Adas Yeshurun in Washington Heights. Rabbi Schwab, was appointed Dayan and later Rav of that community. A member of the Moetzes Gedolei HaTorah he authored *Mayan Bais HaShoeiva* on the Torah and *Megilos*.

Sfas Emes, see Alter, Rabbi Yehuda Leib

Shach, Rabbi Eliezer Menachem Mann (1897-) is *Rosh Yeshiva* of Ponevez and the one of the world's oldest and most revered Torah authorities. Head of the Moetzes Gedolei HaTorah, he is also the author of *Avi Ezri*, a comprehensive multi-volume work on the Rambam.

Shapiro, Rabbi Meir (1887-1933), the Rav of Lublin, Poland, founded Yeshivas Chachmei Lublin. A brilliant and tremendously energetic *Gaon*, he introduced the concept of *Daf Yomi*, the daily Talmudic folio, which has thousands of participants to this very day.

Sherer, Rabbi Moshe (1921-1998) was the President of Agudath Israel of America for the latter half of the Twentieth Century. Ordained at Ner Israel Rabbinical College, and inspired by Rabbi Elchonon Wasserman, Rabbi Sherer was a devoted adherent to the advice of the Council of Torah Sages, during his tenure of leadership at Agudath Israel for nearly four decades.

Shmuelevitz, Rabbi Chaim (1902-1978) was *Rosh Yeshiva* of the Mirrer Yeshiva in Jerusalem, where his brilliant shiurim (Talmudic discourses) and *shmuessin* (ethical talks) were renowned.

Silver, Rabbi Eliezer (1881-1968) was a prominent figure in the emerging American Torah community. A powerful, witty, and brilliant leader, he was Rabbi of Harrisburg, Pennsylvania, and later Rabbi of Cincinnati, Ohio. He was a founder of the Vaad Hatzalah during the Holocaust.

Sofer, Rabbi Moshe (1762-1839) of Pressburg, was the leader of Hungarian Jewry during the emergence of the Reform movement which he battled fiercely. Rabbi Sofer authored numerous works on responsa, Chumash, and Talmud. Many of his works are entitled *Chasam Sofer*, a name by which he was better known.

Soleveitchik, Rabbi Chaim (1853-1918) was the *Rosh Yeshiva* of Volozhin and Rabbi of Brisk. In addition to his brilliant approach to

Talmudic law and reason, he was also known for his extreme piety and saintly nature.

Svei, Rabbi Eliyahu (1923-) is *Rosh Yeshiva* of Talmudical Yeshiva of Philadelphia, a member of the Moetzes Gedolei Torah, and chairman of the Rabbinical Board of Torah U'mesorah. Rabbi Svei was was born in Lithuania andcame to the United States at a young age. He is a disciple of Rabbi Ahron Kotler, *Rosh Yeshiva* of Beth Medrash Govoah, Lakewood, NJ.

Trop, Rabbi Naftali (1871- 1929) was the *Rosh Yeshiva* of the Yeshiva Ohr HaChaim in Slobodka, and later became *Rosh Yeshiva* of the Chofetz Chaim's yeshiva in Radin. His illuminating Talmudic exegesis was published as *Chidushei HaGranat*.

Twerski, Rabbi Mordechai Twerski (1770-1820) of Czernobel, was the author of *Likutei Torah.* A chasidic master, he left eight sons, each a tzaddik in his own right.

Wasserman, Rabbi Elchanan Bunim (1877-1941) was the *Rosh Yeshiva* of Ohel Torah in Baranovitz, Poland. His influence upon students was as far-reaching as the United States, where he visited to raise funds for the yeshiva. Author of the classic works *Kovetz Shiurim* and *Kovetz Ma'amarim*, Rabbi Wasserman, a student of the Chofetz Chaim, was killed by the Nazis in the Kovner (Kounus) Ghetto.

Weinberg, Rabbi Noach (c.1924 -) is the founder and *Rosh Yeshiva* of Jerusalem's Aish HaTorah and its numerous worldwide affiliates. Spearheading the Ba'al Teshuva Yeshiva movement, his influence helped establish hundreds of programs and institutions geared toward reaching unaffiliated Jews and returning them to their heritage.

Yonah, Rabbeinu of Girondi (Gerona) (1180-1263) was the author of *Shaarei Teshuva, Gates of Repentance,* the classic masterpiece of the philosophy and laws of repentance. A leader of medieval Spanish Jewry, and a Teacher of Talmud in Toledo he authored works on both the Talmud and the Torah. Much of his works are lost but they are cited by many of the Talmudic masters of his generation.

Sources

Among the many sources I have consulted during the writing of this book, I gratefully acknowledge the following authors and publishers:

Ayers,Alex, *The Wit and Wisdom of John F. Kennedy*, ©1996, Penguin Books

Baumol, Rav Yehoshua, *A Blaze in the Darkening Gloom*, The Life of Rav Meir Shapiro, zt"l, ©1994, Feldheim Publishers

Boller, Paul F., *Presidential Anecdotes*, ©1981, Oxford University Press

Boller, Paul F., *Congressional Anecdotes*, ©1991, Oxford University Press
Brinkley, David, Everyone is Entiltled to My Opinion, ©1996, Ballantine Books

Bunim, Amos, *A Fire in his Soul: Irving M. Bunim, The Man and His Impact on American Orthodox Jewry*, ©1989, Feldheim Publishers

Eliach, Yaffa, *Hasidic Tales of the Holocaust*, ©1982, Oxford University Press

Fadiman, Clifton, *The Little, Brown Book of Anecdotes*, ©1985, Little, Brown & Co.

Greenwald, Yisroel, *Reb Mendel and His Wisdom: The Enduring Lessons of the Legendary Rosh Yeshiva, Rabbi Mendel Kaplan*, © 1994, Mesorah Publications

Harvey, Paul, *The Rest of the Story*, ©1980, William Morrow & Co.

Himelstein, Shmuel, *Words of Wisdom, Words of Wit*, ©1993, Mesorah Publications

Krohn, Rabbi Paysach J., *The Maggid Series*, ©1987-1996, Mesorah Publications

Raz, Simcha, *A Tzadik in Our Time The Life of Rabbi Aryeh Levin*, ©1976, Feldheim Publishers

Regan, Geoffrey, *Histrionics: A Treasury of Historical Anecdotes*, ©1994, Robson Books

Rosenblum, Yonason, *Reb Yaakov: The Life and Times of HaGaon Rabbi Yaakov Kamenetzky*, ©1990, Mesorah Publications

Schlossberg, Rabbi David J., *Reb Elya:The Life and Accomplishments of Rabbi Eliyahu Lopian*, ©1999, Mesorah Publications

Schwadron, Rabbi Sholom, *Sh'al Avicha*, ©1993, M'chon Da'as

Shapiro, Chaim, *Once Upon a Shtetl: A Fond Look Back at a Treasured Slice of the Jewish Past*, ©1996, Mesorah Publications

Stern, Rav Yechiel Michel, *HaMashgiach D'Kaminetz*, ©1998 Yechiel Michel Stern

Teller, Hanoch, *And From Jerusalem His Word: Stories and Insights of Rabbi Shlomo Zalman Auerbach*, © 1995, NYC Publishing Company

Twerski, Rabbi Dr. Abraham J., *Not Just Stories*, ©1997, Shaar Press

Twerski, Rabbi Dr. Abraham, J., *Generation to Generation*, ©1991, C.I.S. Publications

Twerski, Rabbi Dr. Abraham J., *Do Unto Others*, ©1997, Andrews McMeel Publishing;

Wallach, Sholom, *Shaare Armon*, © 1993, Tevunah Publishers

Weiss, Dr. James David, *Vintage Wein: The Collected Wit & Wisdom of Rabbi Berel Wein*, © 1992, Shaar Press

In addition to those mentioned in the Introduction, and those mentioned in the stories, the author expresses his thanks to the following individuals who have contributed to the weekly *FaxHomily*, and in turn to this volume, with anecdotes, insightful comments, and constructive criticisms.

Rebbitzin Miriam Adahan, Rabbi Sender Laib Aronin, Rabbi Yaakov Beinenfeld, Rabbi Moshe Chopp, Rabbi Yossel Czapnick, Rabbi Shmuel Dishon, Stephen Flatow, Rabbi Yissochor Frand, Adam Parker Glick, Rabbi Heshy Hissiger, Avrohom Chaim Knobel, Rabbi Doniel Neustadt, Rabbi Meir Schiller, Rabbi Sheya Twerski, Rabbi Moshe Weinberger, Rabbi Nisson Wolpin, Rabbi Avraham Biderman, and Rabbi Meir Zlotowitz